# Italian Academy Training Sessions for U11 - U14

## A Complete Soccer Coaching Program from the Italian Serie 'A'

### Written By the
### Soccer Italian Style Coaches

Mirko Mazzantini

Simone Bombardieri

### Published By

# Italian Academy Training Sessions for U11 - U14

## A Complete Soccer Coaching Program from the Italian Serie 'A'

First Published September 2011 by SoccerTutor.com
2nd Edition Published May 2012 by SoccerTutor.com
This 3rd Edition Published Jan 2014 by SoccerTutor.com

Info@soccertutor.com I www.SoccerTutor.com
**UK**: 0208 1234 007 I **US**: (305) 767 4443 I **ROTW**: +44 208 1234 007

**ISBN** 978-0-9566752-1-7

**Authors**
Soccer Italian Style (Mirko Mazzantini and Simone Bombardieri) © 2011

**Edited by**
SoccerTutor.com

**Cover and book design by**
Alex Macrides, Think Out Of The Box Ltd.
email: design@thinkootb.com Tel: +44 (0) 208 144 3550

**Diagrams**
Diagram designs by SoccerTutor.com. All the diagrams in this book have been created using SoccerTutor.com Tactics Manager Software available from
**www.SoccerTutor.com**

Note: While every effort has been made to ensure the technical accuracy of the content of this book, neither the author nor publishers can accept any responsibility for any injury or loss sustained as a result of the use of this material.

# Meet the Coaches of Soccer Italian Style

### Mirko Mazzantini
**"ACF Fiorentina Academy Coach"**

Mirko Mazzantini coached for Empoli FC for 10 years, at almost all the main age groups of the academy level. In 2010 he was then recruited by AFC Fiorentina working with the U14/U15 Academy teams. During the 2010/11 season Mirko won the U15 Italian Academy Serie 'A' championship. UEFA 'B' Coach and author of many coaching publications, articles, books and DVDs.

### Simone Bombardieri
**"Empoli FC Academy Coach"**

Simone Bombardieri played as a player in the Empoli FC club for 5 years. He then started his career as a coach being recruited by Empoli FC where he has been coaching the academy age groups in the last 9 years from U9 – U14. This coming season Simone is in charge of the U15 Academy team. UEFA 'B' Coach and author of many coaching publications, articles, books and DVDs.

# Introduction

## Session 1

| Practice 1 | Passing and Possession Warm-Up | 11 |
| Practice 2 | Coordinated Global Circuit - Technical and Mobilisation | 12 |
| Practice 3 | Passing, Receiving and Creating Space | 13 |
| Practice 4 | Possession and Speed of Play in a Small Sided Game | 15 |
| Practice 5 | Game Situation – Fast Break Attack | 16 |
| Practice 6 | Create and Exploit Numerical Advantage in a SSG | 17 |

## Session 2

| Practice 1 | Passing Combination Warm-Up | 19 |
| Practice 2 | Speed Circuit Training | 20 |
| Practice 3 | 4 v 2 Possession - Passing, Receiving and Speed of Play | 22 |
| Practice 4 | Dynamic Passing and Possession Game | 23 |
| Practice 5 | Dynamic 4 v 4 Possession Small Sided Game | 25 |
| Practice 6 | Quick Transition Play and Finishing in a SSG | 27 |

## Session 3

| Practice 1 | Technical Dribble and Pass Warm-Up | 30 |
| Practice 2 | Football Speed and Strength Tests | 31 |
| Practice 3 | Game Situation – Playing from the Back | 32 |
| Practice 4 | Double 2 v 2 with Drop Deep to Attack in a SSG | 34 |
| Practice 5 | Technical Passing and Shooting | 35 |
| Practice 6 | Dynamic 8 v 4 'Quick Play' Small Sided Game | 36 |

## Session 4

| Practice 1 | Rugby Rules Coordinative Warm-up | 39 |
| Practice 2 | Acceleration and Speed Endurance Training | 40 |
| Practice 3 | Technical Ball Control - Moves / Feints | 42 |
| Practice 4 | Technical Dribbling, Feints and Moves | 43 |
| Practice 5 | Attacking and Defending (Frontal Marking) Drill | 44 |
| Practice 6 | 1 v 1 Duel - Feints, Dribbling and Change of Direction | 45 |

## Session 5

| Practice 1 | Warm-up - Rugby Rules Small Sided Game | 47 |
| Practice 2 | Acceleration, Speed, Agility and Resistance Training | 48 |
| Practice 3 | 1 v 1 Duel - Feints and Dribbling | 49 |
| Practice 4 | Lateral Marking and Forcing Play in 1 v 1 Duel | 50 |
| Practice 5 | Technical Dribbling, Feints and Shooting | 51 |
| Practice 6 | 2 v 2 Tournament Style Small Sided Games | 52 |

# Session 6

| | | |
|---|---|---|
| Practice 1 | Technical 1 v 1 Warm-Up | 54 |
| Practice 2 | Coordinated Global Circuit - Technical Speed and Agility | 55 |
| Practice 3 | Game Situation – Transition Play | 56 |
| Practice 4 | Technical Ball Control and Dribbling Circuits | 58 |
| Practice 5 | Attacking and Defending with Back to Goal | 60 |
| Practice 6 | Game Situation – Collective Tactical Play of Movement | 61 |

# Session 7

| | | |
|---|---|---|
| Practice 1 | Technical Passing and Receiving Warm-Up | 64 |
| Practice 2 | Global Conditioning - Technical, Agility and Endurance | 65 |
| Practice 3 | Ball Possession with Goalkeeper Zones | 66 |
| Practice 4 | Game Situation – Marking from Crosses | 68 |
| Practice 5 | Game Situation – Crossing and Finishing | 69 |
| Practice 6 | Crossing and Finishing in a Small Sided Game | 70 |

# Session 8

| | | |
|---|---|---|
| Practice 1 | Psycho-Kinetics (Think and Act Quickly) + Shooting Accuracy | 72 |
| Practice 2 | Coordination, Agility and Speed Training | 74 |
| Practice 3 | Switching the Play of Attack | 75 |
| Practice 4 | Switching the Play of Attack with Overlap | 77 |
| Practice 5 | 3 v 3 Attacking and Defending Tactical Set Plays | 79 |
| Practice 6 | Possession, Passing Accuracy and Receiving | 80 |

# Session 9

| | | |
|---|---|---|
| Practice 1 | Ball Possession and Quick Transitional Play Warm-Up | 82 |
| Practice 2 | The Yo-Yo Interval Recovery Test | 83 |
| Practice 3 | 1 v 1 Feints and Dribbling (Frontal Marking) | 84 |
| Practice 4 | Getting In-behind the Defence and Attacking on Goal | 86 |
| Practice 5 | Quick Possession and Transition Play to the Striker | 87 |
| Practice 6 | Tactical Flank Play, Crossing and Finishing in a SSG | 88 |

# Session 10

| | | |
|---|---|---|
| Practice 1 | Warm-Up - Transition Play and Heading SSG | 91 |
| Practice 2 | Aerobic Conditioning in a Small Sided Game | 92 |
| Practice 3 | Heading Finishing Accuracy | 93 |
| Practice 4 | Psycho-Kinetics Dynamic Attacking Game | 94 |
| Practice 5 | 3 v 3 Quick Combinations and Finishing in the Box | 95 |
| Practice 6 | Fast Breakaway Small Sided Game | 96 |

# Session 11

| | | |
|---|---|---|
| Practice 1 | Midfielders- Interceptions and 1 v 1's | 98 |
| Practice 2 | Global Conditioning - Technical and Speed of Play | 99 |
| Practice 3 | Centre Backs - Tactical Defensive Positioning | 100 |
| Practice 4 | Game Situation - 3 v 2 Attacking Play | 101 |
| Practice 5 | 6 v 6 Game Situations - Quick Combinations of Play | 102 |
| Practice 6 | Speed of Play and Shooting Small Sided Game | 104 |

# Session 12

| | | |
|---|---|---|
| Practice 1 | Technical Ball Control, Juggling and Volleying | 106 |
| Practice 2 | Anaerobic Power with the Ball | 107 |
| Practice 3 | 1 v 1 Shielding the Ball | 108 |
| Practice 4 | 2 v 1 Attacking and Defending Game | 109 |
| Practice 5 | Psycho-Kinetics (Think and Act Quickly) Possession Play | 111 |
| Practice 6 | Create Space in a Zonal Small Sided Game | 112 |

# Soccer Italian Style Philosophy

Soccer Italian Style was born in 2005. Mirko Mazzantini (ACF Fiorentina) and Simone Bombardieri (Empoli FC) are both professional academy coaches of the Italian Serie 'A'. They have combined due to their great passion for youth development and they have embarked on a joint project that has taken them to various other parts of the world such as the United States, Canada, France and Norway.

The Soccer Italian style philosophy is made up of the principal features of the Italian style series and Mirko and Simone's vast experiences of professional training in Italy and football worldwide. The book outlines a training methodology that is simple and efficient which the authors have personally tested over time throughout their careers in Italy. **They have been highly successful in producing top players who are both technically and tactically astute.**

The success of this program has been demonstrated by the numerous academy victories against the main teams in Italy and European football with far greater resources. Mirko's Under 15 team at Fiorentina won the Italian Academy League in 2010-11 beating teams such as AC MIlan, Inter Milan and Juventus to the title.

Many players who have been trained using this exact program in Italy have gone on to professional careers and have been capped for the Italian national teams in various age groups, where before this was simply not the case.

This book contains 12 training sessions with each session focused on fundamental technical or tactical coaching that is analysed throughout the 6 practices. The 12 sessions have been developed to demonstrate the need of progressions in training, using the basic principle "from simple to complex".

Inside the two volumes there are general team exercises that are useful for all coaches and players in every position, but there are also many specific exercises that are designated for individual roles or positions within a team (e.g. attackers, midfielders or defenders).

Mirko and Simone have a high expertise in technical training and they have developed activities that are open to numerous variations which means that the 12 sessions can be used over and over to make this program of training even more complete.

This passion has driven the pair to "write on paper" what they have learned and experienced up to today, with a great hope that this method will be greatly enjoyed by the readers and used throughout the world to create top quality professional players.

**Soccer Italian Style**
Mirko Mazzantini & Simone Bombardieri

# Session Format

There are at least 6 practices in each of the 12 sessions with some having additional progressions.

**All 12 sessions always start with:**
Practice 1 - Warm-up always with the ball
Practice 2 - Football specific conditioning
Practice 3 - 6 cover both technical and tactical practices.

**Each practice includes clear diagrams with supporting training notes such as:**
- Name of Practice
- Objective of Practice
- Coaching Points of Practice
- Variations or Progression of Practice (if applicable)
- Coaching Points of Practice.

# Key

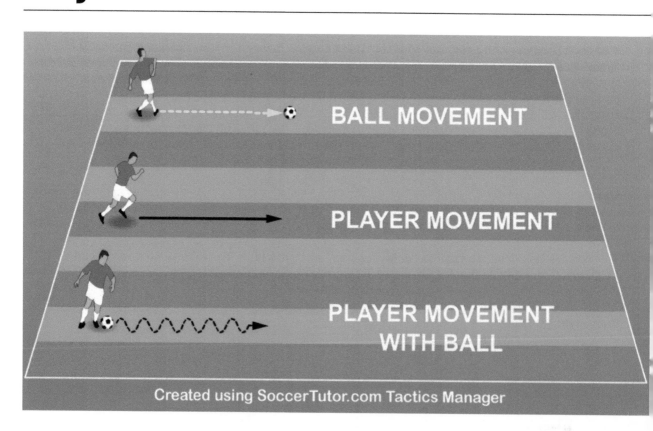

BALL MOVEMENT

PLAYER MOVEMENT

PLAYER MOVEMENT WITH BALL

Created using SoccerTutor.com Tactics Manager

# Session 1

Practice 1     Passing and Possession Warm-Up

Practice 2     Coordinated Global Circuit - Technical and Mobilisation

Practice 3     Passing, Receiving and Creating Space

Practice 4     Possession and Speed of Play in a Small Sided Game

Practice 5     Game Situation – Fast Break Attack

Practice 6     Create and Exploit Numerical Advantage in a SSG

# Passing and Possession Warm-Up

15 Minutes

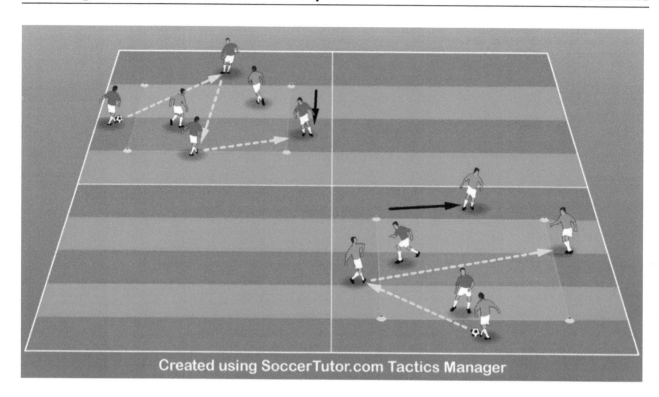

Created using SoccerTutor.com Tactics Manager

## Objective

To develop passing, possession and creating space (unmarking) in a warm-up practice.

## Description

In a square of 5 yards we play 4 v 2.

The four players outside the square have a maximum of 2 touches and must maintain possession playing only from outside of the square.

The two defenders inside the square have to intercept the ball. The player who looses possession ball will change roles to become a defender.

## Coaching Points

1. Create space to find the right position and angle to receive the ball.
2. Improve the speed of play by limiting to 1 touch when possible.
3. It is very important to coach the correct body shape for receiving passes.
4. The 2 defending players must communicate and work together, one closing down the man in possession and the other covering the angle for the pass.

**20 Minutes** — ## Coordinated Global Circuit - Technical and Mobilisation

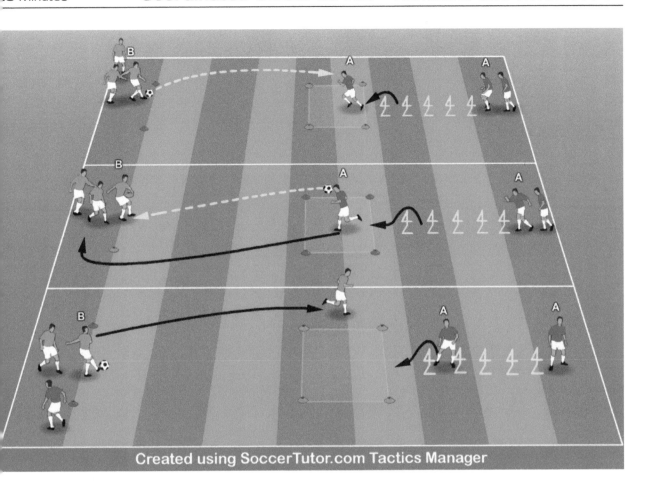

*Created using SoccerTutor.com Tactics Manager*

## Objective
To develop mobilization of the hip and pelvis, especially the lumbar spine that has greater rigidity in players. Global coordination associated with the technical attributes of passing and heading.

## Description
The players work in groups.

**Players (A)** must jump over all the hurdles (40 - 50cm, approximately 15 - 20 inches) in a series of different ways each time; front, back, sideways or a full 360 degree rotation.

The players on the left **(B)** will play a lofted pass into the square of cones for **player A** to head straight back.

**Player A** follows their header sprinting to replace the position **Player B** who does a series of warm up exercises at a relaxed pace to reach **Player A's** starting position.

Exercises should include skips, kicking their legs up back and front and fully extended leg stretches.

# Passing, Receiving and Creating Space

20 Minutes

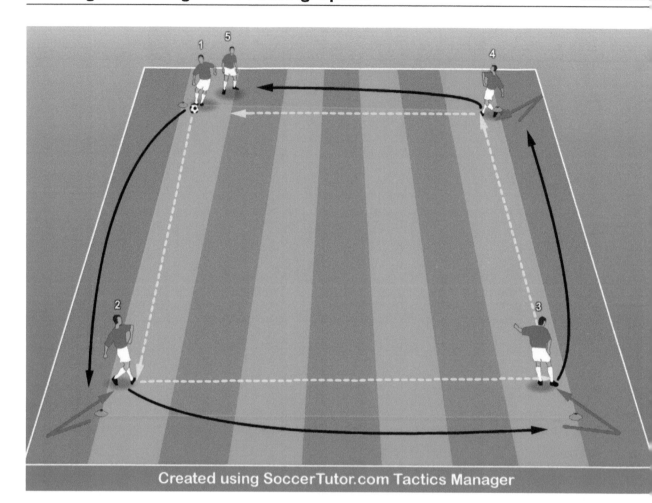

Created using SoccerTutor.com Tactics Manager

## Objective

To develop passing and receiving and creating space (unmarking).

## Description

In squares of 8 yards we play in groups of 5.

There are 2 variations.

### 1st variation (Above Diagram):

Players pass straight and should follow the direction to replace the position of the receiver.

The receiving player must first create space (using the cone as a defender) by checking away before receiving the pass.

The same sequence continues until the coach instructs to switch the direction.

## Passing, Receiving and Creating Space

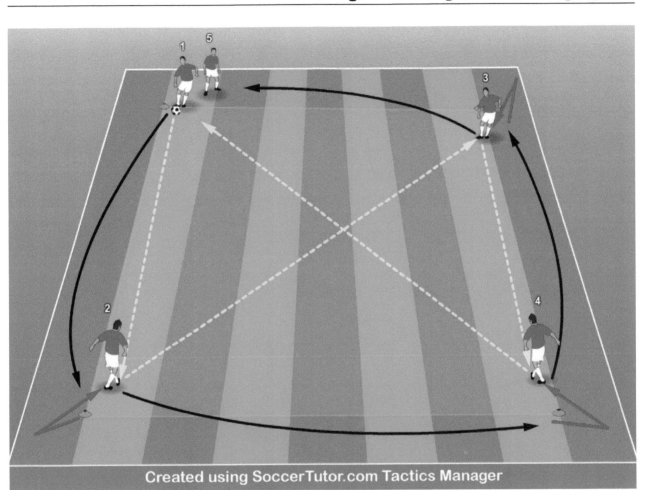

Created using SoccerTutor.com Tactics Manager

**2nd variation (Above Diagram):**
Players pass diagonal and run straight.

## Coaching Points

1.  Improve the speed of play by limiting to 1 touch when it is possible.
2.  Players should time their movement well when creating space. It must be made while the pass is traveling between the previous 2 players.
3.  When creating space, the player should check away with an open body shape before moving to receive the pass.
4.  The correct body shape should be monitored (opening up) and receiving the ball with the back foot (foot furthest away from the ball).

## Progression:

1.  Add an extra ball with 6 players for each group. This way there will be 2 balls going at the same time increasing the speed of play and difficulty.
2.  Coach will call "SWITCH", players have to respond quickly changing the playing direction.

# Possession and Speed of Play in a Small Sided Game

20 Minutes

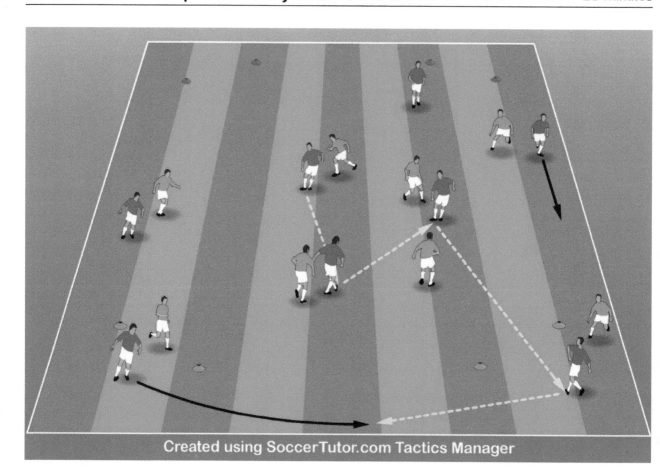

Created using SoccerTutor.com Tactics Manager

## Objective

To develop ball possession, speed of play and creating space.

## Description

In a field area of 30 x 20 yards there are 2 teams of 8 players keeping possession, with both sides defending 2 goals (gates) each.

The objective is to pass the ball through the set of gates directly to a team-mate to score 1 goal.

The players will be limited to 2 touches.

## Coaching Points

1. Movement to create space by losing your marker to receive the pass.
2. Passes must be of high speed.
3. Timing of the runs must be coordinated to the pass.
4. Encourage players to receive passes half-turned. This enables players to develop their awareness which allows for quicker and better decision making.

# Game Situation – Fast Break Attack

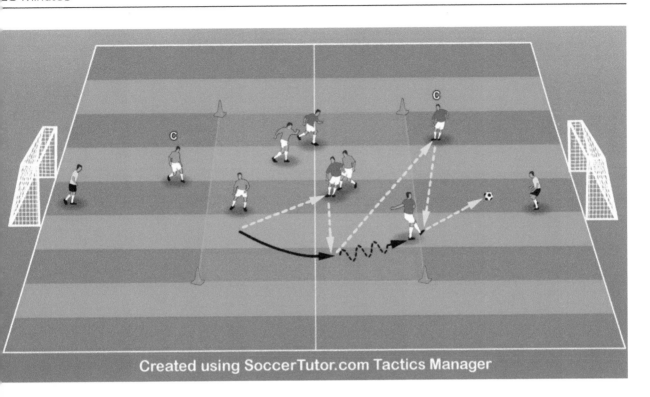

Created using SoccerTutor.com Tactics Manager

## Objective
To develop quick play, breaking from midfield with the aim of finishing on target.

## Description
In a field area of 20 x 20 yards we play 3 v 3 and with a maximum of 2 touches.
Each team has the use of 1 player at the end of the pitch (the Captain), who plays with 1 touch.

The task of each team is to pass the ball to the captain who has 1 touch to lay-off to the player who made the pass, who then shoots on goal.

We play mini-matches of 2 minutes and we rotate the captain. This drill gets players to practice passing in a tight space and develops the ability to receive the ball in a game situation.

## Coaching Points
1. Teach players to angle their body in relation to where the defender is, always protecting the ball.
2. Making your first touch into space, away from the defender.
3. Dragging your marker away and creating space for others to exploit.
4. Awareness and communication to move the ball quickly to the captain.
5. Encourage players to look up to spot that decisive pass.

# Create and Exploit Numerical Advantage in a SSG

25 Minutes

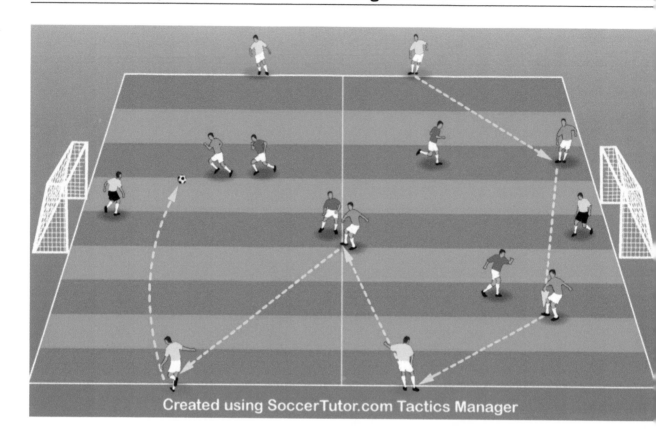

Created using SoccerTutor.com Tactics Manager

## Objective
To create and exploit a numerical advantage and develop fast attacks.

## Description
In a field area of 25 x 15 yards we play 4 v 4 with 2 extra players on each side of the pitch.

The 4 side players play with the team that has possession of the ball helping them maintain it with an 8 v 4 numerical advantage. The players on the field of play are limited to 2 touches, while the side players are reduced to just 1 touch.

This practice develops passing and aims to improve the speed of play. The players learn how to stretch the opposition's inferior numbers to create great space to move the ball forwards quickly.

Every 3 minutes the sides are change, also rotating the side players.

## Coaching Points
1. Play and think quickly.
2. Running into space to receive the ball, fully exploiting the numerical advantage.
3. Analyse the change of the game situation immediately.

# Session 2

Practice 1    Passing Combination Warm-Up

Practice 2    Speed Circuit Training

Practice 3    4 v 2 Possession - Passing, Receiving and
Speed of Play

Practice 4    Dynamic Passing and Possession Game

Practice 5    Dynamic 4 v 4 Possession Small Sided Game

Practice 6    Quick Transition Play and Finishing in a SSG

## Passing Combination Warm-Up

15 Minutes

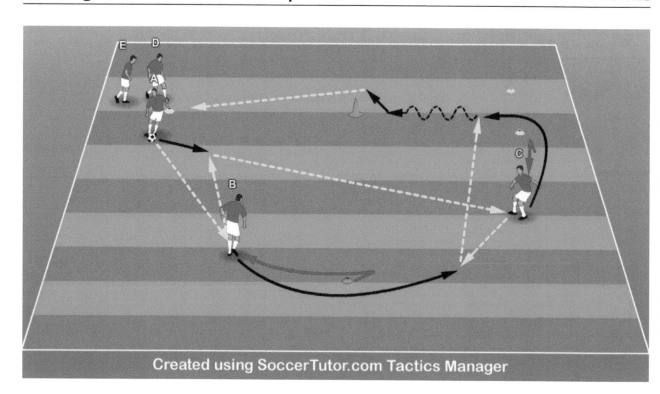

Created using SoccerTutor.com Tactics Manager

## Objective
To develop passing, receiving and movements needed to create space to lose your opponent.

## Description
In a field area of 20 x 20 yards 4 players work in a group practicing passing combinations.

**Player A** passes to **Player B** who has checked to create space from the cone (used as a defender).

**Player B** passes back into **Player A's** path who passes to **Player C** who must check away to create space from the cone and plays into the path of **Player B** who has run round to receive the pass.

**Player B** then passes the ball in front of the two cones (gate) for **Player C** to run onto, dribble past the traffic cone and pass to **Player D**.

**Player D** becomes **Player A**, **A** becomes **B**, **B** becomes **C** and **C** becomes **D**.
The sequence starts again.

## Coaching Points
1. Open body shape - half-turned and receive/pass back with the back foot.
2. Timing of runs - need to be timed well when creating space to receive the pass.
3. When players check to create space from the cone, it should be done at high speed simulating a game situation.
4. Players should be using both feet for all the movements and combinations.

## Speed Circuit Training

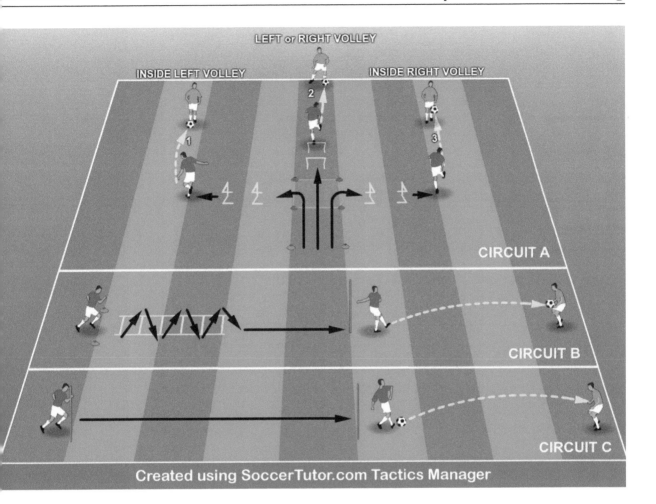

## Objective
To develop football specific speed training whilst working on technical attributes.

## Description
**CIRCUIT A:**
Three players start in between the set of cones. On the coach's command;

**Player 1** sprints into the square, turns left to skip sideways over the hurdles then volleys back to the server with the inside of the left before before returning directly back to the start position.

**Player 2** sprints straight, skips over the hurdles before volleying back with either the left of right foot. Player 2 returns directly back to the start position.

**Player 3** sprints into the square, turns right to skip over the hurdles then volleys with the right foot before returning back to the start position.

All players complete the 3 routes continuously and then exchange with the servers.

# Speed Circuit Training

## Variations:

1. Add full 360 degree rotations for hurdle jumps.

2. Vary passes using in-step, laces and outside of the foot.

### CIRCUIT B:

Players will run through the speed ladder, making steps diagonally across constantly changing direction at 45 degree angles.

The player must then sprint for 3 yards and go round the pole ready to volley the ball back to their teammate or coach who has thrown the ball at waist height for the player.

## Variations:

1. Volley pass with the left foot, right foot and then both in turn.

2. Use the in-step, the laces and then the outside of the foot.

### CIRCUIT C:

The player slips past the pole, then performs a 7 yard sprint and past the second pole. He must then perform the same process as Circuit B with the same variables.

# 20 Minutes

# 4 v 2 Possession - Passing, Receiving and Speed of Play

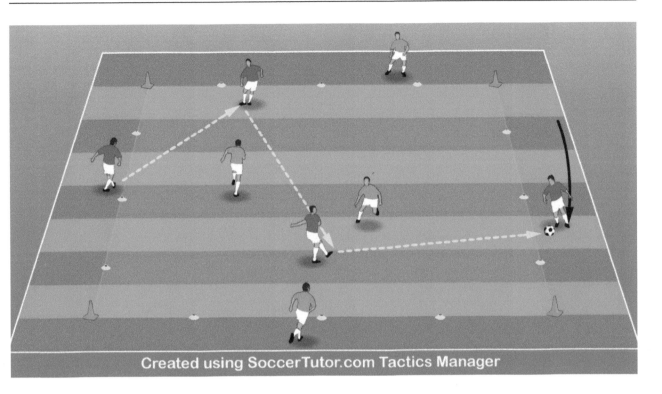

Created using SoccerTutor.com Tactics Manager

## Objective
Developing ball retention: Passing, receiving & losing your marker.

## Description
In a square area of 10-12 yards we play 2 v 2.

Each side has 2 side players who can move up and down their line, but are not allowed to enter the square. This creates a 4 v 2 numerical advantage.

The aim is to maintain possession utilising all 4 players in the team, all of whom are limited to 2 touches.

The aim of the game is to reach 10 passes within your team without the opposition intercepting the ball. The players use the 4 v 2 numerical advantage while in possession.

Every 2 minutes the sides are changed, also rotating the side players.

## Coaching Points
1. All players should open up their body to shape themselves in the direction of their first touch and pass to a teammate.
2. Angle of support - provide support with at least 2 viable passing options.
3. Speed up play: Reduce the time taken between the first touch and the pass.

# Dynamic Passing and Possession Game

20 Minutes

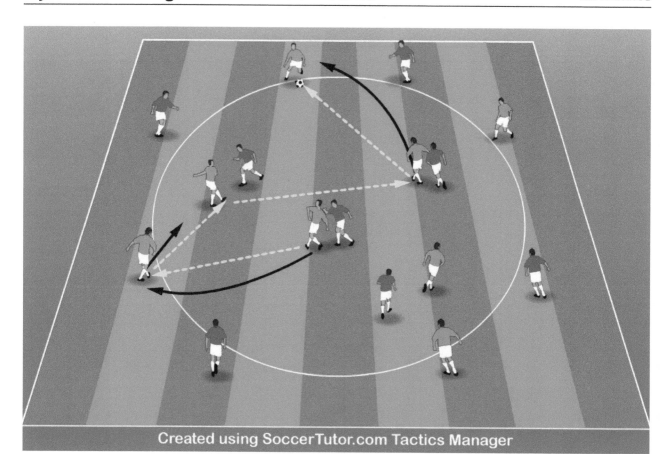

Created using SoccerTutor.com Tactics Manager

## Objective

Practice passing, receiving and creating space (movement to lose opponent).

## Description

In a circular zone of 30 yards diameter, we play 4 v 4. Each side has the use of 4 players outside the area who are awaiting a pass.

1. When a player inside the area completes a pass to a player outside it he follows his pass and takes the place of the receiver.

2. The outside player who has received a pass enters the circular zone and passes to one of his teammates to maintain possession.

3. This process carries on while the team tries to maintain possession of the ball.

## Coaching Points

1. Players should exploit the use of the outside players and the numerical advantage.
2. Make sure the players communicate, clearly calling for the ball after gaining advantageous positions.

## Dynamic Passing and Possession Game

3. All players need to create space for themselves and for team-mates to exploit. This is achieved by checking their runs, runs from outside to in and from inside to out.
4. Body shape should be open - awareness of space and other players is the key in this exercise.
5. If tight situations, the first touch should be away from the defender, with the body creating a barrier between the defender and the ball.
6. Encourage players to use both feet.

# Dynamic 4 v 4 Possession Small Sided Game

20 Minutes

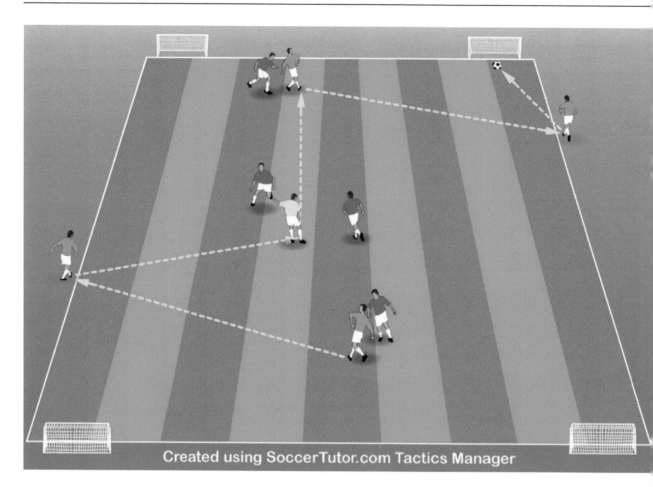

Created using SoccerTutor.com Tactics Manager

## Objective

Developing passing, receiving and possession in a small sided game.

## Description

There is also 1 'Jolly' who will join whichever team has possession of the ball.

The team in possession places the 2 external players wide to the sidelines. The aim here is to use the full width of the pitch to maintain possession.

The defending team may all enter the field of play to prevent the opposition (+ the 'jolly') from advancing up the field and creating opportunities to score.

## Variation

Play with limited touches.

## Dynamic 4 v 4 Possession Small Sided Game

### Coaching Points

1. Create space, losing your marker to receive the pass.
2. Players should look to use the wide players wherever possible to stretch the pitch and drag the defenders away creating vast amounts of space to exploit.
3. Passes must be of high speed and arrive directly at the player's feet.
4. Timing of the runs must be coordinated to the pass.
5. The wide players must make themselves available at all times.

## Quick Transition Play and Finishing in a SSG

20 Minutes

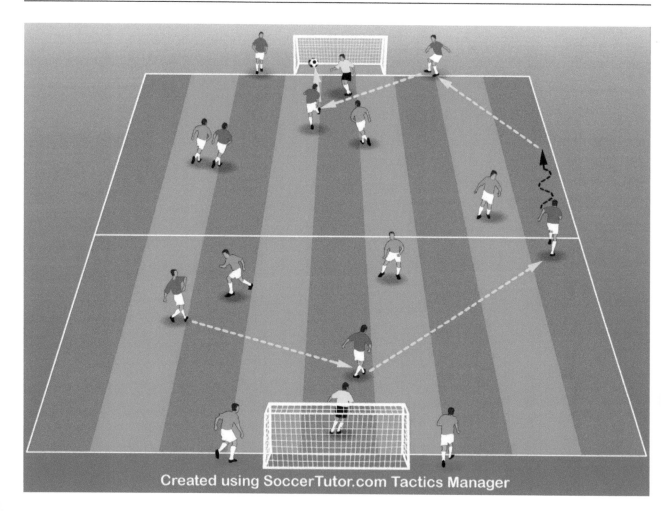

Created using SoccerTutor.com Tactics Manager

## Objective

To develop quick transition play and finishing.

## Description

In a field area of 30 x 20 yards we play 5 v 5.

Each side has the use of 2 external players who are positioned at the end of the pitch either side of the opposition's goal.

The aim is to pass the ball to the external players as soon as possible to create goal scoring chances quickly.

The wide players should maintain good width passing quickly to the external players to create fast transitions of play.

## Quick Transition Play and Finishing in a SSG

## Coaching Points

1. The wide players should be encouraged to dribble the ball up the flank to complete a pass to the external players.
2. Use the full width of the pitch.
3. The focus should be to get the ball up the pitch as quickly as possible and develop wing play.
4. Passes must be of high speed and accurate.
5. Timing of the runs must be coordinated to the pass.
6. Encourage players to receive passes half-turned. This enables players to develop their awareness which allows for quicker and better decision making.

# Session 3

Practice 1     Technical Dribble and Pass Warm-Up

Practice 2     Football Speed and Strength Tests

Practice 3     Game Situation – Playing from the Back

Practice 4     Double 2 v 2 with Drop Deep to Attack in a SSG

Practice 5     Technical Passing and Shooting

Practice 6     Dynamic 8 v 4 'Quick Play' Small Sided Game

15 Minutes                    **Technical Dribble and Pass Warm-Up**

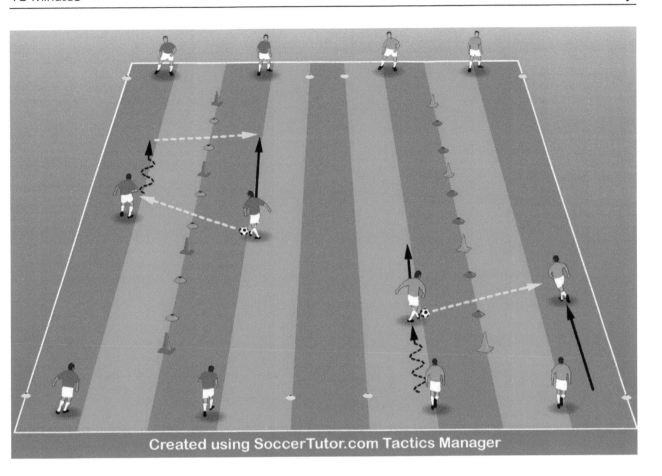

Created using SoccerTutor.com Tactics Manager

## Objective
Developing technical attributes such as dribbling and passing in a warm-up.

## Description
Players perform a series of passing in pairs. They must dribble and then pass through the cone gateways.

Start off at a steady pace and increase the speed once major muscle groups have been warmed-up and stretched.

The pass should be guided into their partner's path and the player should quickly sprint to the next position to receive the pass.

Fun - The pairs can compete with the adjacent group to who can finish the fastest.

## Coaching Points
1. Dribble the ball close to feet so you're able to make the pass early.
2. Speed up play: Reduce the time taken between the first touch and the pass.
3. Make sure the 1-2 combination is quick and sharp.
4. Timing of the runs must be coordinated to the pass.

# Football Speed and Strength Tests

20 Minutes

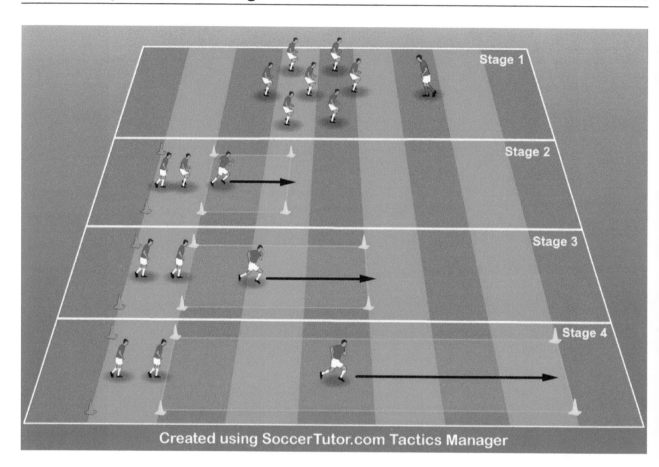

Created using SoccerTutor.com Tactics Manager

## Objective

To evaluate the physical performance of the players for speed and strength.

## Description

### Stage 1:

One group of players are doing squat jumps with the coach making sure they are done properly and monitoring their performance. The coach will count how many the players achieve 30 in a minute.

### Stage 2 - 4:

The other players are working on their speed;

They are timed for a 5 metre sprint, 10 metre sprint and a 20 metre sprint.
This tests players acceleration and speed over short distances.

The athletic performance of the players is recorded including marks for speed and strength.

2 minutes: Recovery rest before moving on to the next stage.

## Game Situation – Playing from the Back

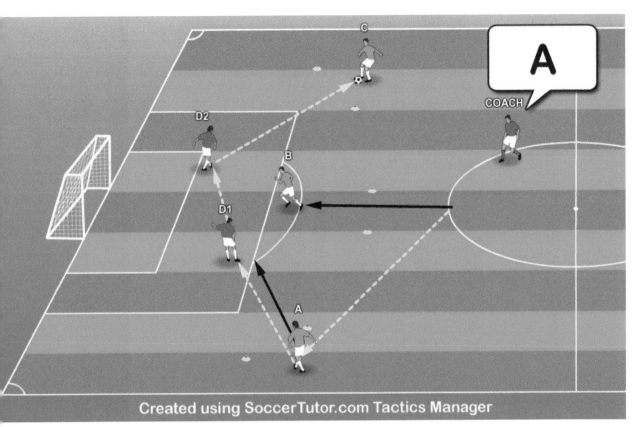

Created using SoccerTutor.com Tactics Manager

## Objective
A technical and tactical drill, to coach the central defenders on passing out from the back.

## Description
Players A, B and C exchange passes until the coach signals A or C to pass through the cones (gate) to one of the central defenders (D1 and D2).

The player follows his pass closing down the defenders, along with B who runs through the central gate to intercept the pass or tackle the central defender.

Player D1 who receives the pass is limited to 2 touches and passes to partner D2 who needs to have moved behind the line of the ball and into space.

The sequence is completed when player D2 passes through the set of cones to player C.

# Game Situation – Playing from the Back

## Coaching Points

1. Before the the central defender receives the ball from player A or C, the central defending partner must create space by dropping back quickly behind the receiving player.
   This creates space making it easier to switch the play and also makes it more difficult for the defenders to get anywhere near the ball.
2. The speed of play should be as in a real game.
3. The pass to the full back should be at pace and accurate.

# Double 2 v 2 with Drop Deep to Attack in a SSG

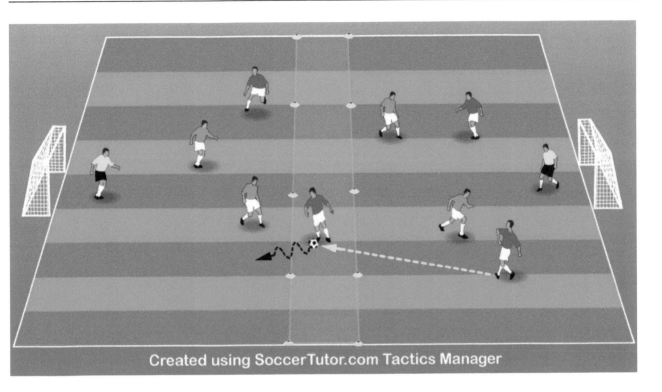

Created using SoccerTutor.com Tactics Manager

## Objective
To develop the use of attackers dropping deep in the hole to start of an a attack.

## Description
In a field area of 30 x 20 yards we divide the pitch in two with a neutral zone of 5 yards in the middle and play 4 v 4.

Inside each half we play 2 v 2. Only one player can enter the neutral zone. The player's team must have possession in the other half to enter the zone, where you are free and unmarked.

When the attacker receives the ball in the neutral zone he aims to overcome the challenger of the defender and get a shot on goal.

## Coaching Points
1. Create space to find the right position on the field to receive the ball.
2. Players need to have their heads up at all points to spot their teammates dropping into the neutral zone.
3. Get the players to vary the feints and moves to beat, making sure they attack the space in behind the defenders.
4. Quick feet and explosive speed are needed to beat an opponent to create a chance to score.
5. Encourage players to receive passes half-turned. This enables players to develop their awareness which allows for quicker and better decision making.

# Technical Passing and Shooting

20 Minutes

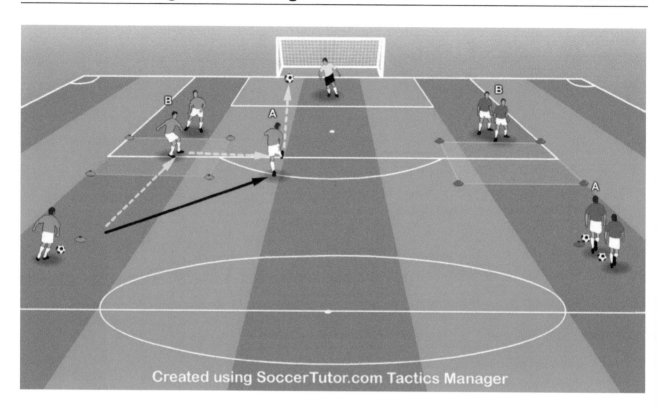

Created using SoccerTutor.com Tactics Manager

## Objective
To develop passing, give and go, setting up play with back to goal and shooting.

## Description
Two groups compete against each other trying to score the most amount of goals.

**Player A** passes to **Player B**, who meets the pass lays the ball off to the edge of the box. **Player A** must sprint to receive the ball in his path to take a shot at goal.

**Player A** will join the position of **Player B** after taking his shot and **Player B** runs to the starting position of **Player A** after making their pass

## Coaching Points
1.    Player A's pass must be of high speed.
2.    Player B must check to create space and meet the pass.
3.    Player B's lay off must weighted well and timed to meet the run and in front of the player A making it easier to strike first time.
4.    Get the players to make a feint / move before executing the shot.
5.    This exercise should be practiced using both feet and rotating the sides.

25 Minutes

# Dynamic 8 v 4 'Quick Play' Small Sided Game

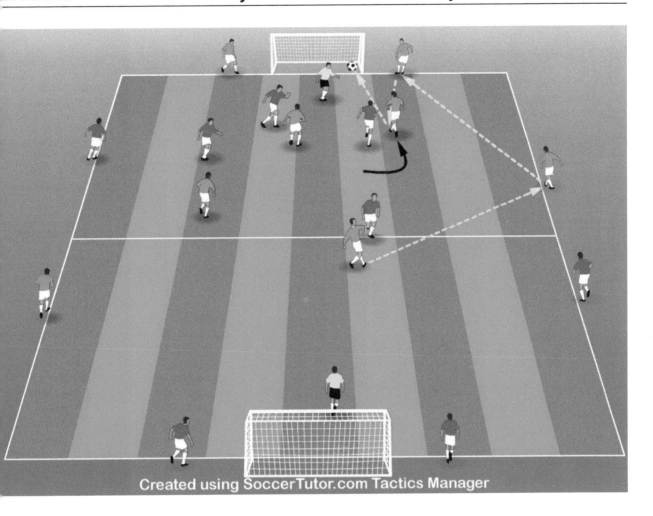

Created using SoccerTutor.com Tactics Manager

## Objective

To develop quick play and utilise wide positions for attacking.

## Description

In a 40 x 30 field area we play 4 v 4 with each side having 4 extra side players, 1 player on each side of the pitch and 2 players at the end of the pitch either side of the opposition's goal.

The team in possession attacks with an 8 v 4 numerical advantage and should aim to get the ball wide as soon as possible utilising all external players.

The players inside the field are limited to 2 touches, with the external players having unlimited touches.

Change the roles every 2 minutes.

## Progression

For more advanced players limit the external players to 1 touch.

# Dynamic 8 v 4 'Quick Play' Small Sided Game

## Coaching Points

1. Create space to find the right position on the field to receive the ball.
2. The players need to make runs from deep to receive the ball from the external players.
3. Timing of runs is essential to finish the chances created by the players at the end of the pitch.
4. Passes should be made to the side players as often as possible, stretching the width of play and utilising the numerical advantage.

# Session 4

Practice 1    Rugby Rules Coordinative Warm-up
Practice 2    Acceleration and Speed Endurance Training
Practice 3    Technical Ball Control - Moves / Feints
Practice 4    Technical Dribbling, Feints and Moves
Practice 5    Attacking and Defending (Frontal Marking) Drill
Practice 6    1 v 1 Duel - Feints, Dribbling and Change
              of Direction

# Rugby Rules Coordinative Warm-up

15 Minutes

Created using SoccerTutor.com Tactics Manager

## Objective

To develop coordinative skills such as creating space behind the ball, switching play, executing feints/moves whilst running with the ball.

## Description

In a field are of 30 x 30 yards we play 5 v 5 with rugby rules. All play is done so with the hands and with a rugby ball if available.

The players have to throw all passes backwards.

All space is to be achieved by running with the ball, with the aim of reaching the end zone.

## Coaching Points

1. Create receiving option by dropping back behind the ball.
2. Run forward at every opportunity.
3. The exercise shows the players how and when to embark on individual movements with the ball to beat an opponent.
4. Individual action should sometimes be used to break through the lines of midfield or defence.

## Acceleration and Speed Endurance Training

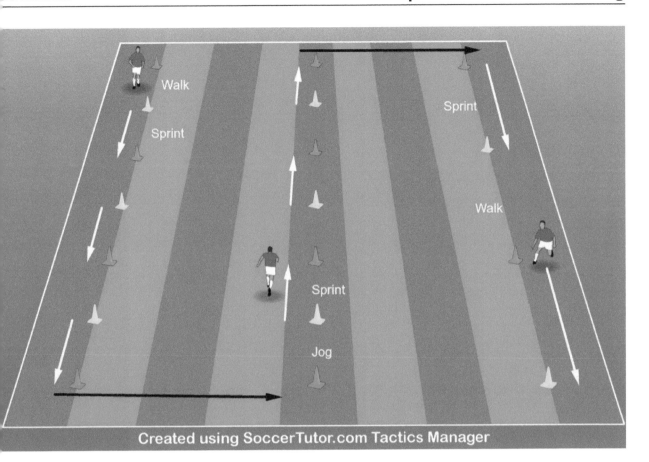

Created using SoccerTutor.com Tactics Manager

## Objective

Two circuit drills to improve acceleration and speed endurance.

## Description

Players work on developing their speed and acceleration. The focus is on explosive movement from a standing position.

There are 3 lines of cones that the players use in a circuit. The first 2 lines, the cones are 5 yards apart and in the third line the cones are 10 yards apart.

1.  The players walk for 5 yards and then sprint for 5 yards in sequence.

2.  The players run slowly (jog) and then sprint for 5 yards in sequence.

3.  The players sprint for 10 yards, stop and walk to the next cone and sprint for the final 10 yards to complete the circuit.

All these exercises can be done with a ball.

# Acceleration and Speed Endurance Training

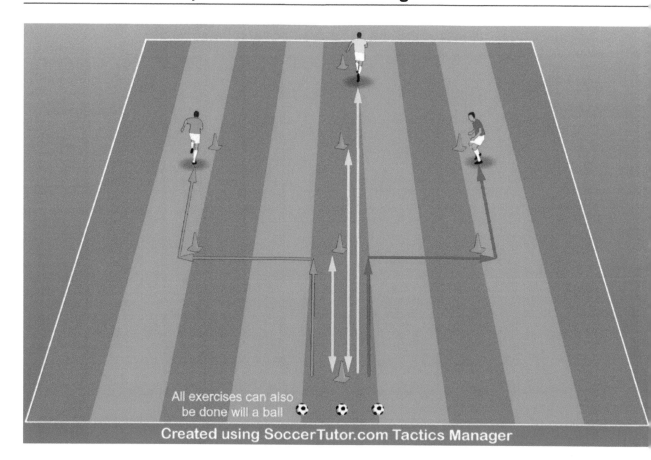

All exercises can also
be done will a ball

Created using SoccerTutor.com Tactics Manager

**Circuit 2 (Above):**

## Description

The players work on their acceleration and speed endurance. Again in this second exercise with three different routes to follow. All the cones are 5 yards apart.

## Route 1 (LEFT):

The player sprints to the first cone, turns and sprints to the cone to the left and then sprints to the final cone.

## Route 2 (STRAIGHT):

The player sprints to the first cone and sprints back to the starting point.
The player then sprints to the second cone and sprits back to the starting point.
To complete the route the player sprints 15 yards to the third cone.

## Route 3 (RIGHT):

The player uses side-steps to get to the first cone, turns and side-steps to the cone on the right and then side-steps to the final cone.

All these exercises can be done with a ball.

15 Minutes

## Technical Ball Control - Moves / Feints

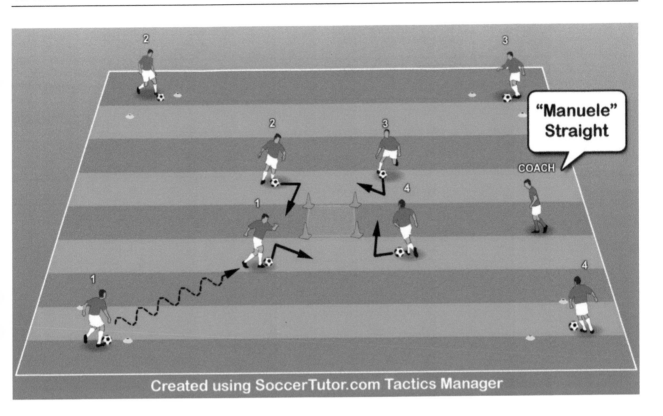

Created using SoccerTutor.com Tactics Manager

## Objective
To develop ball control and practicing different attacking moves / feints.

## Description
In a square of approximately 10 yards we place a circle or in this case position cones in the centre. Players are separated into groups in the corners of the square.

On the coaches command, players dribble towards the centre of the square perform a feint before taking the ball away to the LEFT, RIGHT, RETURN or STRAIGHT to the opposite end.

The different feints and change of position is pre-determined by the coach.

## Coaching Points
1. Keep the ball close to the feet.
2. Make many touches with the ball.
3. Dribbling with the ball should be done with soft touches.
4. Move/feint – exaggerate the move making a sharp movement in a different direction.

# Technical Dribbling, Feints and Moves

**20 Minutes**

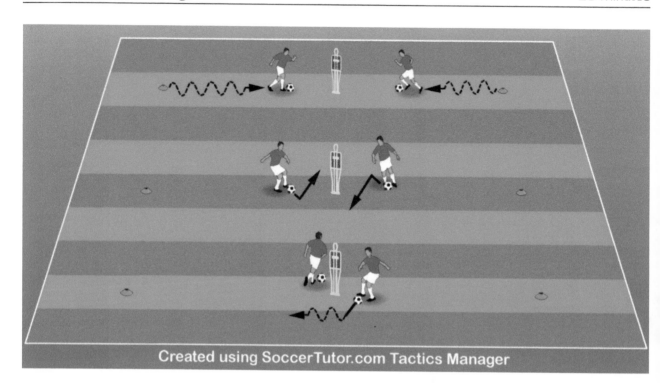

Created using SoccerTutor.com Tactics Manager

## Objective

To develop technical ball control such as dribbling and the executions of various feints / moves.

## Description

This practice is in pairs. The players should be at a distance of 10 yards from each other with a mannequin or cone positioned n the middle of them.

The 2 players perform a feint at the same time of which the coach has predetermined turning in opposite directions.

## Coaching Points

1.  Keep the ball close to the feet.
2.  An exaggeration of the feint is needed as they guide the ball either side of the central cone.
3.  The use of many feints should be used, as well varying the dribbling, such as 2 left foot touches, 2 right, 2 left etc.

## Attacking and Defending (Frontal Marking) Drill

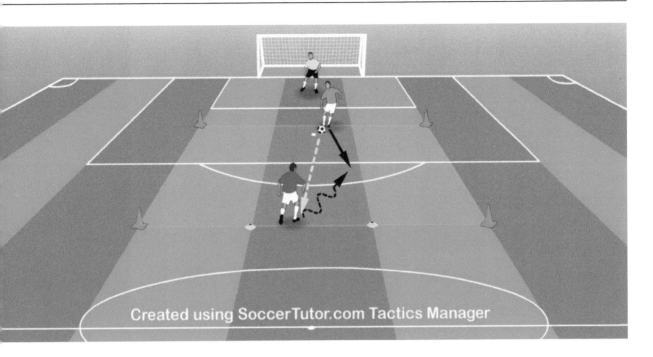

Created using SoccerTutor.com Tactics Manager

## Objective
To develop frontal marking and improve attacking moves as well as close ball control.

## Description
At the edge of the penalty area the defender passes to the attacker and then follows his pass getting in the position to frontal mark his opponent.

The attacking player, after receiving the ball will dribble the ball at the defender attempting to perform a move or feint to beat him and get a shot on goal.

## Coaching Points
1. The defender needs to assess the opponent's speed.
2. The defender should slow down before approaching the attacker.
3. The defender must always have one foot in front of the other in position to half turn to follow the attacker's movement in either direction.
4. The defender should direct the attacker away from goal or onto their weaker foot.
5. The attacker needs to keep the ball very close to their feet.
6. It is important to pay attention to the defender's positioning and exploit any weakness.

# 1 v 1 Duel - Feints, Dribbling and Change of Direction

20 Minutes

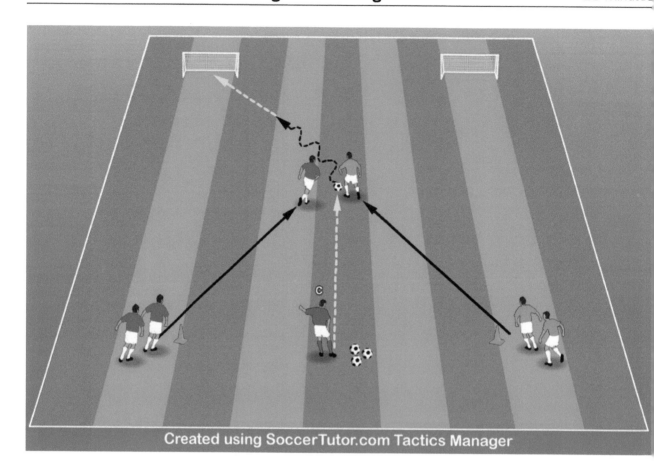

Created using SoccerTutor.com Tactics Manager

## Objective

To develop ball control, dribbling, feints and change of direction in a 1 v 1 duel.

## Description

In a field area of 20 x 15 yards the players compete in 1 v 1 situations.

The coach kicks the ball to the centre of the field. The first player to reach the ball becomes the attacker and aims to score in 1 of the 2 goals.

If the defender manages to tackle or intercept the ball he becomes the attacker.

The use of two goals in this exercise increases the options for changes in direction and different feints.

## Coaching Points

1. The attacker needs to use his body as a barrier between the defender and the ball to protecting it.
2. The attacker needs to keep the ball close their feet using feints and quick change of direction when needed to get away and score.

# Session 5

Practice 1    Warm-up - Rugby Rules Small Sided Game

Practice 2    Acceleration, Speed, Agility and Resistance Training

Practice 3    1 v 1 Duel - Feints and Dribbling

Practice 4    Lateral Marking and Forcing Play in 1 v 1 Duel

Practice 5    Technical Dribbling, Feints and Shooting

Practice 6    2 v 2 Tournament Style Small Sided Games

# Warm-up - Rugby Rules Small Sided Game

15 Minutes

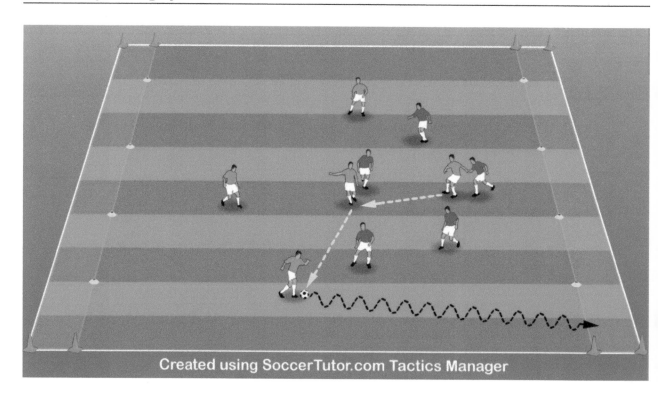

Created using SoccerTutor.com Tactics Manager

## Objective

To develop supporting and creating space behind the ball, as well as switching play, and dribbling and running with the ball.

## Description

In a field area of 30 x 30 yards we play 5 v 5 with the aim of entering into the endzone.

The same rugby rules are used (can only pass backwards) but all play is with the feet.

The only way to gain ground forwards is by running with the ball and dribbling.

## Coaching Points

1.   Players need to provide support (at least 2 options) behind the ball at all times.
2.   Encourage players to beat the opponent using different feints / moves.
3.   If there is limited space on one flank, look to switch the play to create the space to penetrate forward.

## Acceleration, Speed, Agility and Resistance Training

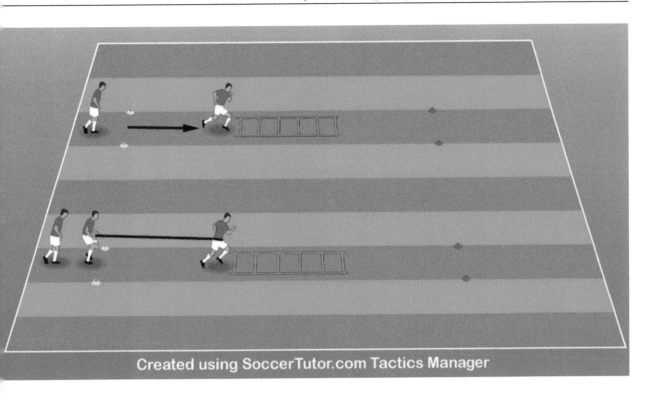

Created using SoccerTutor.com Tactics Manager

## Objective
To develop, acceleration speed, coordination, and agility (quick feet).

## Description
Players work on developing their speed and acceleration. The focus is on explosive movement from a standing position.

**Ladder Exercise 1:**
The first player simply uses a speed ladder using quick feet and landing their toes in between each rung.

You can vary the sequences:
   • Two step touches between each rung.
   • Sideways left
   • sideways right
   • Etc...

**Ladder Exercise 2:**
The second player does the same while their teammate holds a speed bungee which is attached to them to create resistance while sprinting.

# 1 v 1 Duel - Feints and Dribbling

20 Minutes

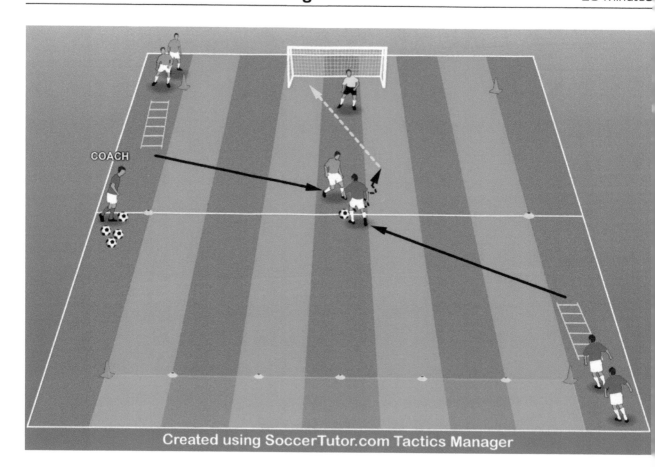

Created using SoccerTutor.com Tactics Manager

## Objective

To develop feints and dribbling in 1 v 1 situations.

## Description

In a field area of 20 x 15 yards two players play against each other in a 1 v 1 practice.

On the coaches signal both players execute fast steps through the speed ladder and then sprint to the centre of the field to gain control of the ball placed there by the coach.

First to the ball becomes the attacker who attempts to beat the defender and shoot at the goal past the goalkeeper.

The defender has to attempt to win the ball. If successful, his objective is to score in a goal by dribbling within the bottom end-zone.

## Coaching Points

1. The players need to demonstrate explosive acceleration.
2. Players need to keep the ball close to their feet.
3. The attacker should try to get a shot on goal as quickly as possible.

**15 Minutes**

# Lateral Marking and Forcing Play in 1 v 1 Duel

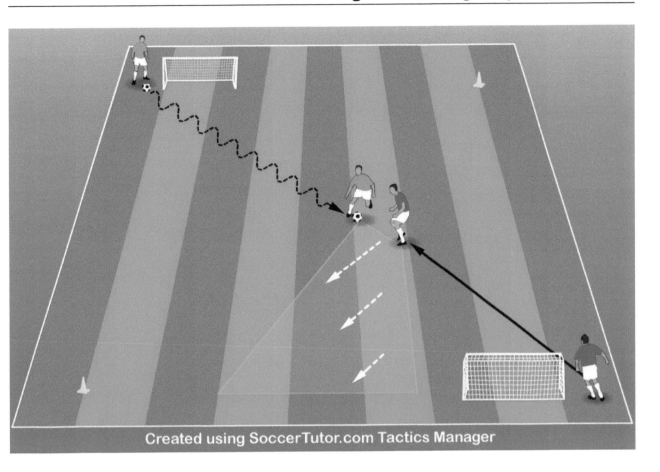

Created using SoccerTutor.com Tactics Manager

## Objective

To develop defensive lateral marking; forcing the attacker away from goal.

## Description

In a field area of 20 x 20 yards, two goals are positioned diagonally on opposite sides of the pitch.

The attacker runs with the ball with the task of scoring in the opposition's net.

The defender has to move forward quickly and face up the attacker to reduce his space and guide him into the zone away from the goal area neutralising the danger.

## Coaching Points

1. The defender needs to close the angle for the attacker.
2. The defender must always have one foot in front of the other in the jockey position.
3. The defender should direct the attacker away from goal into the zone shown, away from danger.
4. Defenders should be patient, stay on their feet and only attempt to challenge for the ball when a clear opportunity arises.

# Technical Dribbling, Feints and Shooting

15 Minutes

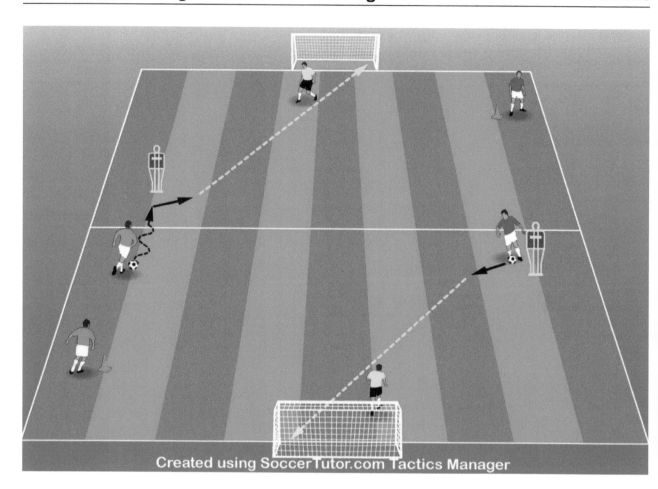

Created using SoccerTutor.com Tactics Manager

## Objective
To develop ball control, dribbling, feints and shooing.

## Description
In a field area of 30 x 30 yards two teams play against each other for how many goals they can score past the goalkeepers.

The players dribble to the mannequin (or cone) and shape their body to perform a feint (varied by the coach) past the mannequin followed with a shot at goal.

Switch the mannequins (or cones) the the opposite side to shoot with the left foot.

## Coaching Points
1. The feint / move should be exaggerated with a radical change of direction with the players making sure to drop their shoulder.
2. Make sure the players imagine the mannequin to be an opposing player and treat them as such.
3. This exercise should be done at full dribbling speed.

# 2 v 2 Tournament Style Small Sided

Created using SoccerTutor.com Tactics Manager

## Objective
To develop ball control in a 2 v 2 situation.

## Description
In areas of 20 x 10 yards teams play 2 v 2 in a round robin tournament.

To score a goal a player has to stop the ball with his sole on the goal line.

The mini-matches last about 2 minutes and then the teams rotate to play against another pair.

Variation: The goal is only valid after successfully beating an opponent with a feint / move.

## Coaching Points
1. Making your first touch into space, away from the defender.
2. Angle of support of team-mate should be behind and in front of the ball.
3. Encourage players to beat their opponent.

# Session 6

Practice 1    Technical 1 v 1 Warm-Up

Practice 2    Coordinated Global Circuit - Technical Speed and Agility

Practice 3    Game Situation – Transition Play

Practice 4    Technical Ball Control and Dribbling Circuits

Practice 5    Attacking and Defending with Back to Goal

Practice 6    Game Situation – Collective Tactical Play of Movement

15 Minutes

# Technical 1 v 1 Warm-Up

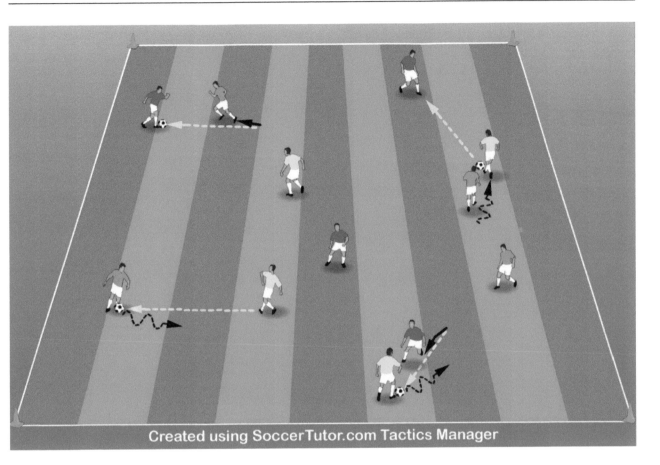

Created using SoccerTutor.com Tactics Manager

## Objective
To develop feints and moves to and player awareness.

## Description
In a square of 20 x 20 yards there are 3 teams of at least 4 players and 4 balls.

The players with possession of the ball pass to other players of a different colour who automatically becomes passive defenders.

The player who receives the ball becomes the attacker and has to beat the defender before searching for a player that is available with a different colour to pass the ball.

The sequence continues.

## Coaching Points
1. An advancement from using mannequins; the players practice their feints on a passive defender.
2. The players should vary the feints outlined by the coach.
3. The defender simply uses frontal marking without touching the player.

## Coordinated Global Circuit - Technical Speed and Agility

20 Minutes

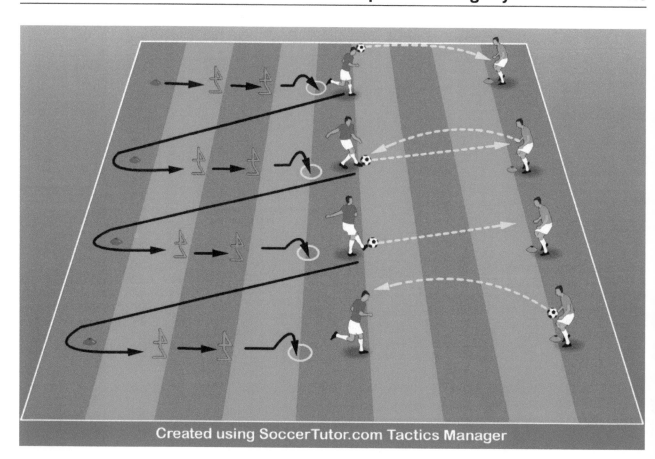

Created using SoccerTutor.com Tactics Manager

## Objective

To develop speed, agility and technical attributes. This is global training that combines technical attributes as well as conditioning qualities.

## Description

The player runs from the first cone and jumps over the two hurdles and into the ring.
A teammate will be ready waiting to throw the ball up for the player to head the ball straight back to them. The player then sprints round to the second cone.

The player repeats the process as done in the first stage but this time volleys the ball back with his right in-step. The player then sprints round to the third cone.

The player repeats the process again but this time volleys the ball back with his left in-step. The player then sprints round to the fourth and final cone.

The player repeats the process again but this time heads the ball back to his coach or teammate. This concludes the full circuit.

Change next 4 players. 6-8 repetitions each.

## Game Situation – Transition Play

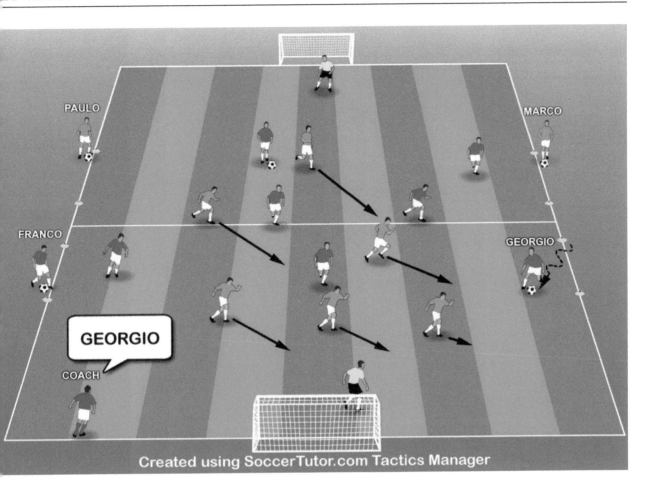

Created using SoccerTutor.com Tactics Manager

## Objective

To develop team tactics in transition play and coping with numerical disadvantages.

## Description

In a large field area the size of goal area to goal area 2 teams play 7 v 7. Each team has 2 side players in the opposition's half.

Inside the field everyone should be set up in their positions until the coach calls out a name of one of the side players. The player who is called out quickly reacts by dribbling the ball at the opposition defence creating a breakaway for his team to attack and score.

The defending team has to adapt immediately making sure to drop back and cover the space as a team to defend their goal.

## Coaching Points

1. The attackers must advance quickly at a high pace to make use of the numerical advantage and create a chance on goal.

# Game Situation – Transition Play

2.  The defending team must tuck in, moving towards the side of the pitch where the wide player is attacking.
3.  As the team shifts over it closes the space in which the attacking team can play.
4.  If the player in possession is forced wide and the other players are marked well the attack should be nullified.

20 Minutes

# Technical Ball Control and Dribbling Circuits

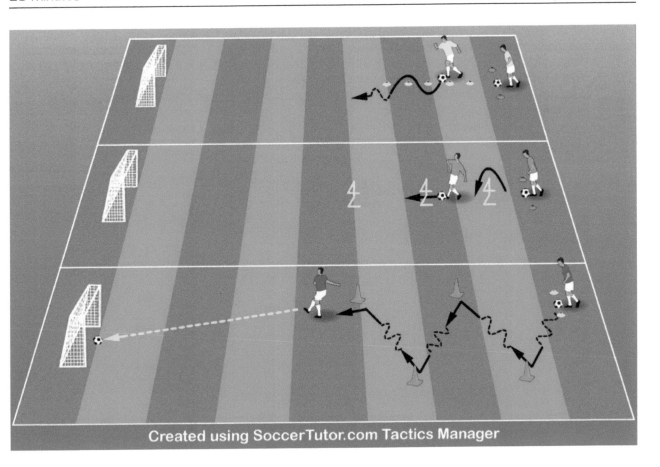

Created using SoccerTutor.com Tactics Manager

## Objective
To develop the technique of ball control and dribbling with quick changes of direction.

## Description
The team works in 3 groups and will rotate.

**Circuit 1:**
In the first section the players dribble the ball through the cones using two touches with alternative feet; right, then left. The player then takes a shot at the goal.
Variations: Dribble with one foot. Outside of feet only.

**Circuit 2:**
In the second section the player guides the ball through the hurdles and jumps over them. The player then takes a shot at goal.

**Circuit 3:**
In the third section the players dribble the ball towards the cones and quickly change direction with a feint at a 45 degree angle to the next cone and does this twice more before taking a shot at goal.

# Technical Ball Control and Dribbling Circuits

## Coaching Points

1. In the first section it is necessary to have a good control of the ball (soft touch in speed) with the aim of transferring the ball through the cones by using the right foot and then the left foot and so on.
2. Slightly bend knees and keep the ball near the feet.
3. In the second section it is important to keep close control of the ball when guiding it under the hurdles.
4. The jumps over the hurdles should be high with legs tucking up.
5. In the third section keep low with sharp changes of direction.

15 Minutes

## Attacking and Defending with Back to Goal

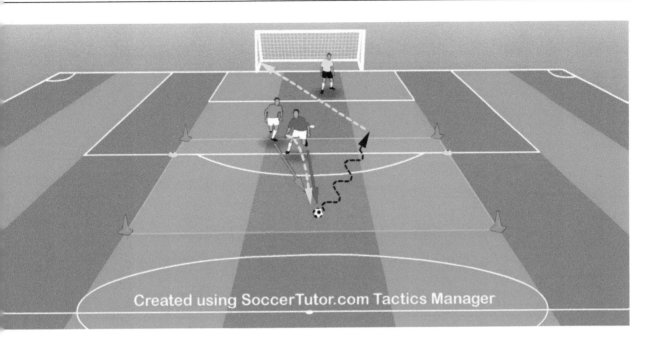

Created using SoccerTutor.com Tactics Manager

## Objective
Attacker: To develop dribbling, feints and turning.
Defender: To develop back marking, preventing the attacker from turning.

## Description
In a area the width of the 6 yard box, there is 1 attacker and 1 defender.

On the coaches signal the attacker throws the ball a distance of 10 yards. This begins a 1 v 1 situation with both players having their backs to goal.

The attacker will attempt to turn and attack the space behind the defender and score in the goal past the goalkeeper. The defender must maintain sufficient pressure on the attacker not letting him turn and making sure not to commit a foul.

## Coaching Points
1. The attacker needs to protect the ball using his body as a barrier between the defender and the ball.
2. When turning the ball should be kept the maximum distance away from the defender.
3. The attacker needs to keep the ball close to their feet.
4. It is important to coach the correct distance for the defender to be, who must be close enough to apply pressure, while also covering the space in behind.

# Game Situation – Collective Tactical Play of Movement

25 Minutes

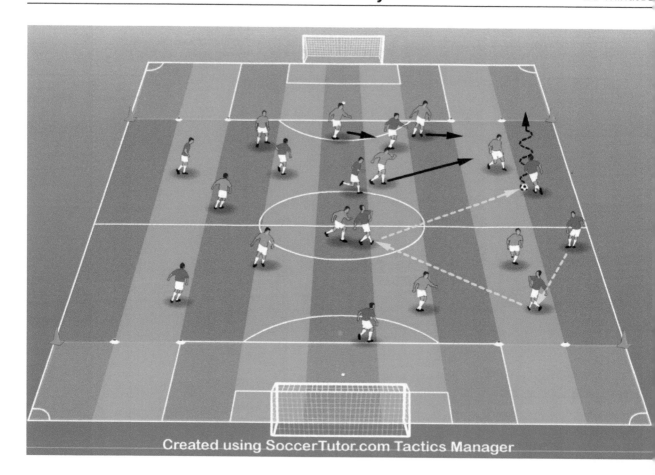

Created using SoccerTutor.com Tactics Manager

## Objective

To develop the collective tactical play of movement in the phase of possession and movement in the phase without possession.

## Description

In a field area of we play a match of 10 v 10 to the limit of the penalty areas. If you haven't got that many players, then simply play with the numbers you have, I.e. 7 v 7 etc.

The aim of the team in possession is to advance the ball past the last line of defence and the line of cones at the end of the pitch.

As play develops the coach observes the player positioning and movements. Stops the play and corrects the mistakes.

## Variation:

Shorten the area of play to put the players under more pressure.

## Game Situation – Collective Tactical Play of Movement

### Coaching Points

1. Encourage the players to dribble past their opponents.
2. Players should stick close and mark 1 player each in this restricted area.
3. Players retain the responsibility in their area of the field.
4. The players need to be taught to move as a collective defensive unit to prevent attacking movement.
5. Using 11 a side tactical positions, the players' ball control is tested in this smaller area, making them used to being under immense pressure when in possession of the ball.
6. Body shape should be open to maximise player awareness when team is in possession and not in possession.

# Session 7

Practice 1     Technical Passing and Receiving Warm-Up

Practice 2     Global Conditioning - Technical, Agility and
               Endurance

Practice 3     Ball Possession with Goalkeeper Zones

Practice 4     Game Situation – Marking from Crosses

Practice 5     Game Situation – Crossing and Finishing

Practice 6     Crossing and Finishing in a Small Sided Game

20 Minutes

## Technical Passing and Receiving Warm-Up

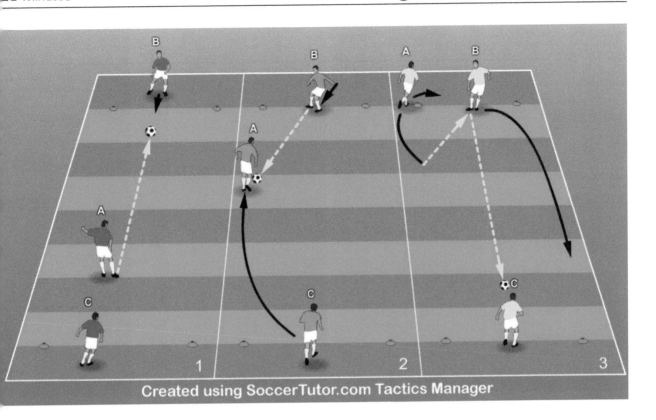

Created using SoccerTutor.com Tactics Manager

## Objective
To develop passing and receiving as well as creating space and player awareness.

## Description
The team works in groups of 3's at a distance of about 20 yards.

**Player A** passes the ball with the inside of the foot to **Player B** and moves to receive the ball at an angle.

**Player B** moves to meet the ball and pass to **Player A** who passes straight back then moves behind **B** to change places. **Player B** then passes long to **Player C**

**Player B** then follows the direction of the ball but at an angle ready to receive a pass back from **Player C**. The same sequence continues.

## Coaching Points
1. Players on the outside should move to meet the ball and also step back at an angle to the left or right to create space before receiving the pass back.
2. The middle player should receive a pass at an angle and with the back foot, this automatically opens the body shape on the half-turn enabling to see both players on the outside. This develops good player awareness.
3. Timing of movement and communication is important.

# Global Conditioning - Technical, Agility and Endurance

20 Minutes

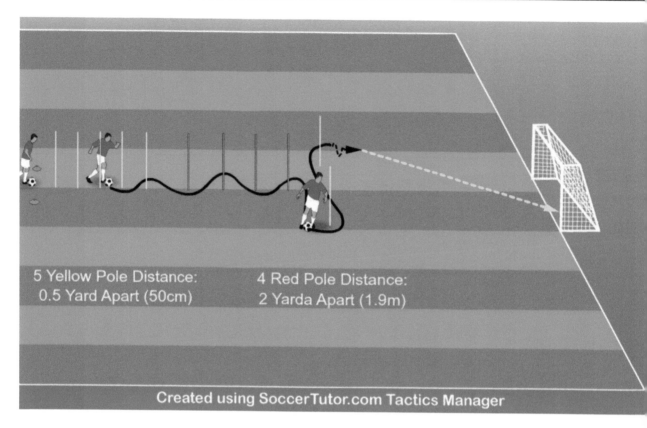

5 Yellow Pole Distance:
0.5 Yard Apart (50cm)

4 Red Pole Distance:
2 Yarda Apart (1.9m)

Created using SoccerTutor.com Tactics Manager

## Objective
To develop player endurance and agility as well as developing technical attributes such as ball control, dribbling and shooting.

## Description
Within half a pitch, the players dribble in and out of each pole.

The first 5 poles are ½ yard apart and the other poles are 2 yards apart.

The varied pole distances simulate game situations having to adapt from short to longer strides when dribbling with the ball.

After dribbling the ball round the 10 poles the player dribbles around the two angled poles in a figure of 8 before taking a shot on goal.

## Coaching Points
1. The changes of direction should be sharp with a drop of the shoulder.
2. The intensity and speed should be high with the player using both feet and all parts of the foot.

20 Minutes                    **Ball Possession with Goalkeeper Zones**

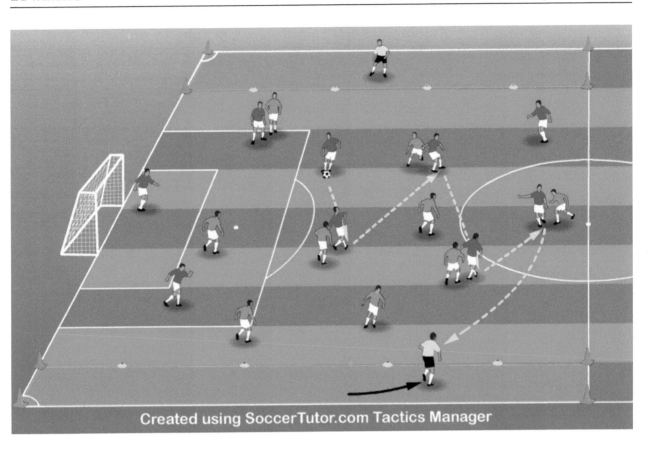

Created using SoccerTutor.com Tactics Manager

## Objective
To develop ball possession and depth of play.

## Description
In half a pitch 2 teams play 10 v 10. If you haven't got that many players, then simply play with the numbers you have, I.e. 7 v 7 etc.

The goalkeepers play in a zone at the end of the pitch. A goal is achieved when a player completes a lofted pass successfully into the goalkeeper's hands.

Variable: We can create a minimum number of passes required before the lofted pass to the goalkeeper.

## Coaching Points
1. Movement to create space by losing your marker to receive the pass.
2. Encourage players to receive passes half-turned. This enables players to develop their awareness which allows for quicker and better decision making.
3. Encourage players to switch the play in order create opportunities to pass to the goalkeeper.

# Ball Possession with Goalkeeper Zones

4. The first touch should be away from the defender, with the body creating a barrier between the defender and the ball.
5. Monitor passing technique, making sure the non-striking leg is slightly bent and the foot is placed next to the ball.

## Game Situation – Marking from Crosses

Created using SoccerTutor.com Tactics Manager

## Objective
To develop defensive marking from crosses.

## Description
Inside the penalty area there is a defender positioned to prevent an attacker from an attempt at goal.

The wide players cross the ball in for the players who are positioned at the edge of the box to run on to and attack for an attempt at goal.

## Coaching Points
1. The defenders must be aware that not only to concentrate on the ball but also to pay attention to the attacker movements too.
2. It is important to coach the correct body shape, so open to see the ball and attacker as well as the correct distance between them and the attacker.
3. The defender must anticipate the area the player will attack and cover the run.
4. With eyes on the ball and staying close to their man the defender must maintain a strong position to clear the ball away.

# Game Situation – Crossing and Finishing

20 Minutes

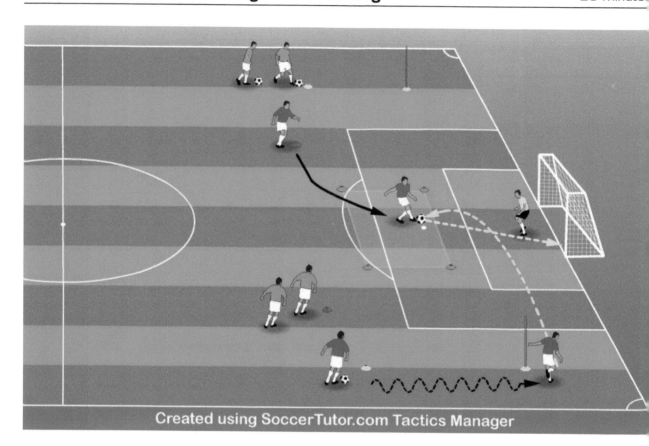

Created using SoccerTutor.com Tactics Manager

## Objective

To develop crossing technique and tactical attacking movements.

## Description

Two teams of at least 4 players. The wide players start from the cone and guide the ball round the pole and execute a cross arriving in the square cone area.

The other player, positioned at the edge of the box moves into the cone square to execute an attempt on goal, which if scored will be worth 1 point. If the player scores from a volley or header, it will be worth 2 points.

## Coaching Points

1. Players attacking the cross must not make their run too early. This will prevent the ball going behind them.
2. The attacker needs to anticipate the delivery of the cross and focus of connecting with the ball.
3. The player crossing should approach the pole with at least a yard distance to the side and then arch the run to make it easier to cross the ball.

## Crossing and Finishing in a Small Sided Game

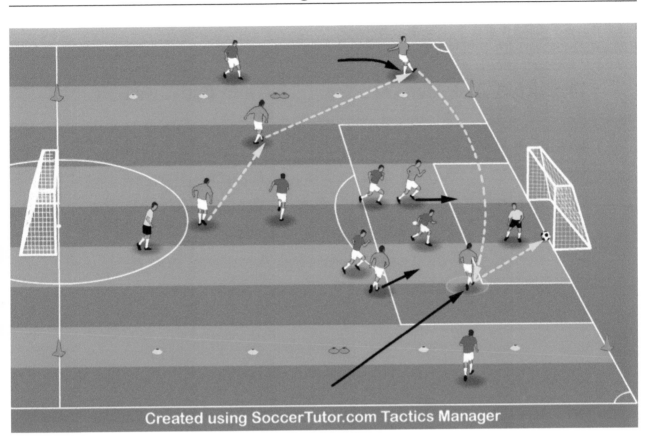

Created using SoccerTutor.com Tactics Manager

## Objective

To develop switching play, using width, crossing, finishing and tactical attacking movements in a small sided game.

## Description

In a half a pitch we play a match 6 v 6. We arrange 2 outside tracks in which 2 wide players of each team are placed, 1 to the right and 1 to the left, that can not disturb each other or be disturbed. The wide players play with a maximum of 3 touches and the goal counts double if there is an assist from a wide player. If there is a cross the opposite wing/back (wide player) can cut in and attack the cross.

## Coaching Points

1. Players should aim to get the ball to the wide players quickly.
2. Players need to time their runs just before the wide player strikes the ball making sure they are attacking the ball in front of them and it not behind them.
3. The attacking players need to communicate and co-ordinate themselves to attack different areas of the box to maximise the danger in the box.
4. Attacking different zones spreads out the defenders creating a greater opportunities to score (near, far post, middle and edge of the box).

# Session 8

Practice 1     Psycho-Kinetics (Think and Act Quickly) +
               Shooting Accuracy
Practice 2     Coordination, Agility and Speed Training
Practice 3     Switching the Play of Attack
Practice 4     Switching the Play of Attack with Overlap
Practice 5     3 v 3 Attacking and Defending Tactical Set Plays
Practice 6     Possession, Passing Accuracy and High Ball
               Reception

## Psycho-Kinetics (Think and Act Quickly) + Shooting Accuracy

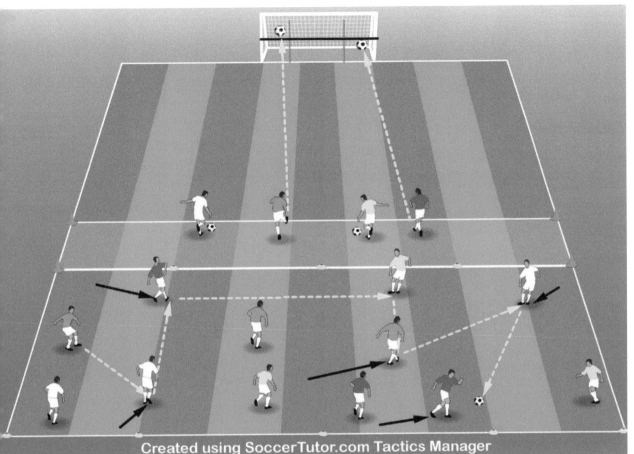

Created using SoccerTutor.com Tactics Manager

## Objective

To develop player awareness and to think and act quickly using Psycho Kinetics. The second fun practice works on shooting technique and accuracy.

## Description

The team is divided into two groups.

**The first group** is split up into 4 groups of 3 colours (3 Blue - 3 red - 3 White - 3 Yellow). Dictated by the coach, players have to pass in a particular colour sequence. I.e. Red - White - Blue - Yellow. The sequence continues until the coach changes it.

**The second group** - At random, the coach calls one player colour from each group to practice their shooting technique and accuracy. From 20 yards, the goal is divided into 4 sections with tape and/or boundary poles.

This provides challenging targets for the players to aim at. The players will vary their technique using the instep, laces and the outside of the foot.

# Psycho-Kinetics (Think and Act Quickly) + Shooting Accuracy

## Coaching Points

First Group (Psycho-Kinetics):

1. Encourage players to think and play quickly selecting the right pass before receiving the ball.
2. Correct body shape (open on the half-turn) and positioning is important to know where the next pass is going.

Second Group (Shooting):
1. Practice various types of shot; laces, inside of the foot, outside.
2. Progress the players from kicking a stopped ball to striking a moving ball.
3. This exercise is designed to be a fun start to a session which practices the accuracy of shooting.

20 Minutes

# Coordination, Agility and Speed Training

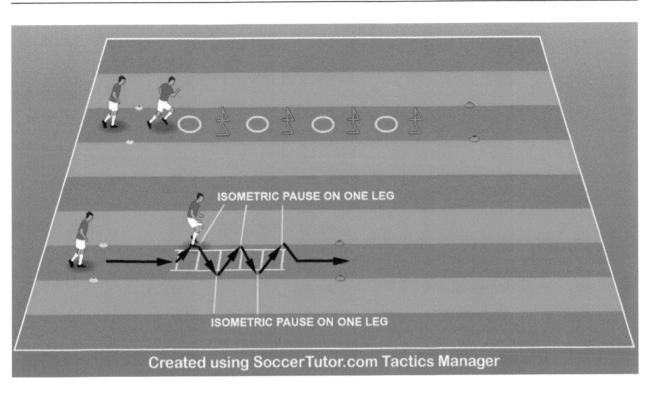

ISOMETRIC PAUSE ON ONE LEG

ISOMETRIC PAUSE ON ONE LEG

Created using SoccerTutor.com Tactics Manager

## Objective
To develop, coordination, agility and speed training with two football specific exercises.

## Description
This practice has two different exercises.

**The first exercise:**
The player steps one foot inside the speed rings and jumps over the 50 cm hurdles.

**The second exercise:**
The player works through the ladder at 45 degree angles and must pause on one leg for 2 seconds at the sides. This is called "Isometric Pause" which will improve acceleration and speed.

# Switching the Play of Attack

15 Minutes

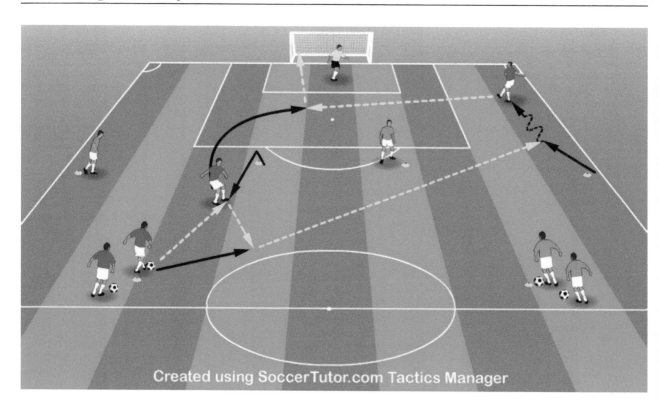

Created using SoccerTutor.com Tactics Manager

## Objective

To develop combination play and switching the play when attacking forward.

## Description

In half a pitch, we work with 3 players.

The central midfielder (CM) passes the ball to the forward (F) who must check his run before meeting the ball to pass/set the ball back to the CM. The CM moves inside and switches the play with his first touch to into the path of the wide player.

The forward turns and makes a run to meet the cross from the wide player. The drill is completed with an attempt on goal from the forward who attacks the near post or the central midfielder who makes a run to the back post.

This should be practiced on both sides of the pitch.

## Coaching Points

1. The forward must check to create space before receiving the pass from the CM.
2. The forwards lay off needs to be in front of the central midfielder so they can make a quick switch of play pass to the wide player.

## Switching the Play of Attack

3.  The wide player should decide early where to cross the ball.
4.  The forward and the central midfielder should attack different areas; front post and near post.
5.  The runs from deep need to be well timed to meet the cross and attack it.

# Switching the Play of Attack with Overlap

15 Minutes

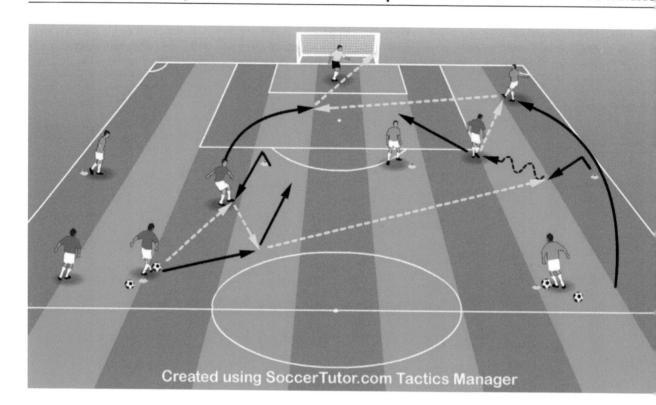

Created using SoccerTutor.com Tactics Manager

## Objective

To develop combination play and switching the play and overlapping when attacking forward.

## Description

As the previous practice we progress with 4 players.

The central midfielder (CM) passes the ball to the forward (F) who must check his run before meeting the ball to pass/set the ball back to the CM. The CM moves inside and switches the play with his first touch to into the wide player who must first create space by checking his run before receiving the pass.

The wide player dribbles inside to create the space for full back making an overlapping run from deep. The wide player plays the ball into the path of the full/wing back and executes a cross.

The practise ends when the forward and the 2 midfielders attacking the cross.

## Coaching Points

1.  The forward must check to create space before receiving the pass from the CM.
2.  The forwards lay off needs to be in front of the central midfielder so they can make a quick switch of play pass to the wide player.
3.  The wide midfielder must imagine using the movement inside to drag a defender away to create space for the overlapping full back.

### Switching the Play of Attack with Overlap

4. The full back should communicate to the the wide player when to release the pass on the overlap so the pass is in front.
5. The runs from deep need to be well timed to meet the cross and attack the ball.

## 3 v 3 Attacking and Defending Tactical Set Plays

20 Minutes

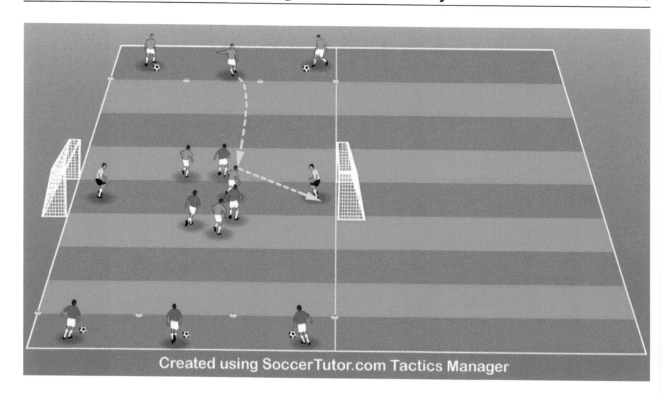

Created using SoccerTutor.com Tactics Manager

## Objective

To develop attacking and defending set plays from mid-air deliveries into the box.

## Description

A goal is moved to the edge of the penalty area and 3 players from each team are positioned by the sideline to cross the ball into the area.

Inside the area we play 3 v 3. The coach assigns which team is defending and which team is attacking to create marking situations typical for set plays.

Variation: Teams can score in either goal from the side players of the same team.

## Coaching Points

1. The attacker needs to make a run across the face of the defender anticipating the delivery of the ball.
2. The jump needs to be timed just before the arrival of the ball reaching the highest possible point when it arrives.
3. The defender must mark the player tightly with body shape slightly open to the ball as well as see and feel the attacker.
4. It is important to coach the correct distance for the defender to maintain between them and the attacker.
5. With eyes on the ball and staying close to their man the defender must maintaina strong position to clear the ball away.

## Possession, Passing Accuracy and Receiving

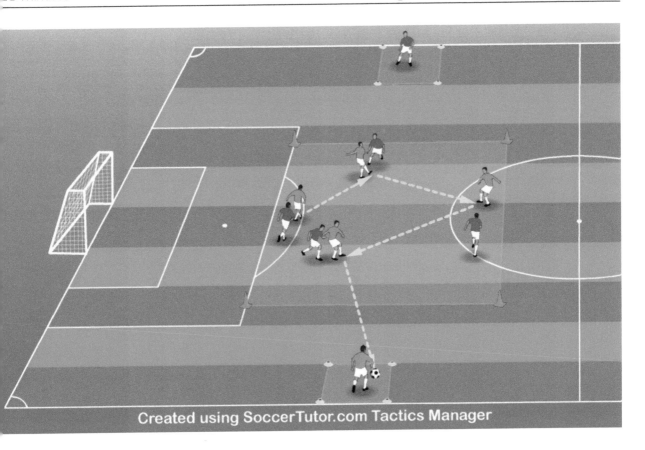

Created using SoccerTutor.com Tactics Manager

## Objective
To develop ball possession, passing accuracy and receiving from low to aerial balls.

## Description
In a field area of 30 x 20 yards we play 4 v 4.

An target player for each team is positioned in a 5 yard square approximately 10 yards from the end of the pitch.

The aim of a team within the field is to make a set amount of passes pre-determined by the coach and then try to execute a pass to their target player. A point is scored when the target player successfully receives the pass.

## Coaching Points
1. Open body shape to see all of the playing options
3. If marked, create space to get away from marker.
2. Teach the players that shifting the ball out wide can relieve the pressure of ball possession and help create good opportunity to pass to the target player.

# Session 9

Practice 1    Ball Possession and Quick Transitional Play
              Warm-Up

Practice 2    The Yo-Yo Interval Recovery Test

Practice 3    1 v 1 Feints and Dribbling (Frontal Marking)

Practice 4    Getting In-behind the Defence and Attacking
              on Goal

Practice 5    Quick Possession and Transition Play to Forward

Practice 6    Tactical Flank Play, Crossing and Finishing in
              a SSG

### 15 Minutes

## Ball Possession and Quick Transitional Play Warm-Up

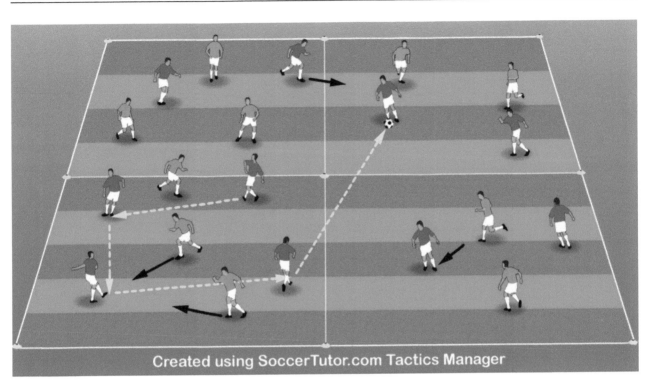

Created using SoccerTutor.com Tactics Manager

## Objective
To develop ball possession passing, receiving, and transitional play.

## Description
We divide an area the size of half a pitch into 4 sections. We play 10 v 10 with players free to move into each sector with the freedom to create a numerical advantage.

The teams aim is to complete 5 consecutive passes (depending on the ability) in a particular sector and then quickly transition the play to a teammate in a different sector.

A point is scored every time a transition of play is succeeded.

## Coaching Points
1. Open body shape to see all playing options.
2. Speed of play is crucial as there is an overload of players.
3. There needs to be active movement to create space and receive passes in this small area.
4. As this is also a warm-up exercise, all players need to keep moving.

# The Yo-Yo Interval Recovery Test

15 Minutes

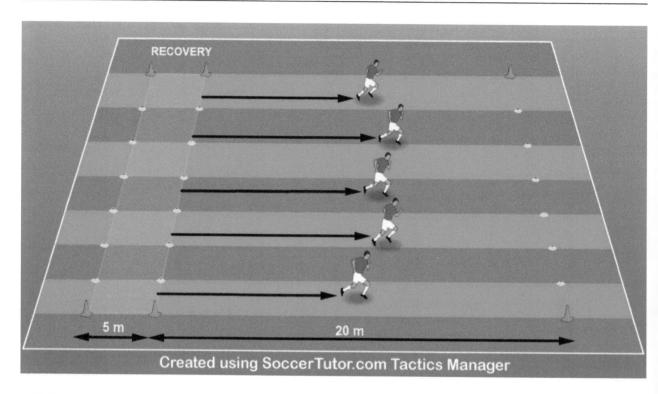

Created using SoccerTutor.com Tactics Manager

## Objective

To develop football specific conditioning using the Yo-Yo Interval test which evaluates the players ability to repeatedly perform intervals over a prolonged period of time.

## Description

Although the Yo-Yo test is conducted using a recording, you can also perform it without it.

This version of the Yo-Yo Interval test last for a total of 12 minutes.

Use cones to mark out three lines as per the diagram above; 20 meters and 5 meters apart for the recovery rest.

The players starts on the middle line, and begin running 20m and back again within 15 seconds. The players then walk/slowly jog in the recovery 5m zone for 15 seconds.

The same procedure is repeated for 12 minutes. The coach will keep control of the timings instructing the players.

15 Minutes

# 1 v 1 Feints and Dribbling (Frontal Marking)

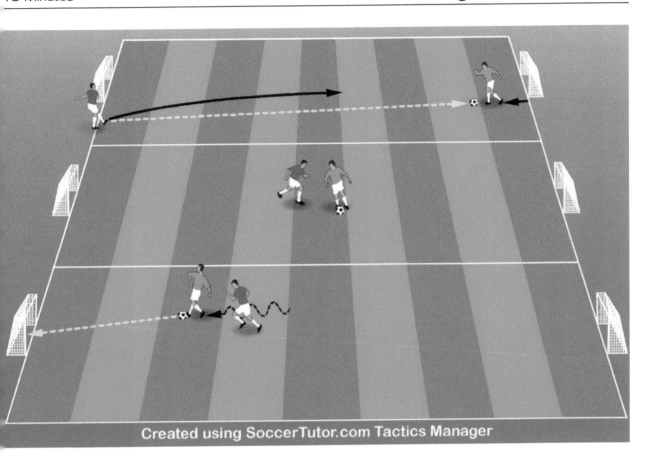

Created using SoccerTutor.com Tactics Manager

## Objective
To develop feints and dribbling as well frontal marking in 1 v 1 situations.

## Description
In a field area of 20 x 10 yards two players play against each other in a 1 v 1 duel.

The first player passes the ball directly to his opposite number who receives the pass moving forward.

When the player receives the ball he dribbles at the player with the objective of scoring in the small goal. If the defender wins the ball and scores in the opposite goal, he has the right to a bonus penalty kick.

The players execute 3 attacks each and then take their penalty kicks afterwards.

This can be used as a tournament where the winners and losers play against each other.

## Coaching Points
1.  The attacker needs to dribble the ball quickly and perform a feint and quick change of direction to be successful and beat their opponent in this narrow area.

# 1 v 1 Feints and Dribbling (Frontal Marking)

2.  The defender needs to press forward standing the right distance away from the attacker in the jockey position.
3.  The defender must try to guide the attacker wide and onto their weaker foot.
4.  The timing of the tackle must be well thought out, pouncing at the right moment when the attacker has limited space.

## Getting In-behind the Defence and Attacking on Goal

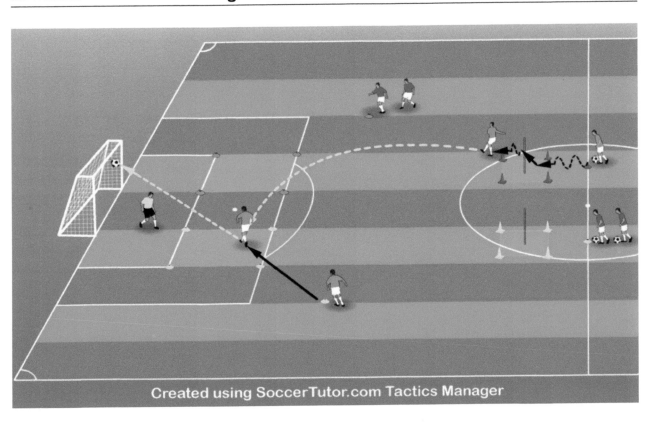

Created using SoccerTutor.com Tactics Manager

## Objective

To develop midfield creative play and getting in-behind the defense. Also works on forward movement and receiving aerial passes and finishing on goal.

## Description

In half a pitch 2 sets of forwards/wingers are positioned 5 yards away from the edge of each box. 2 sets of midfield players are positioned on the half-way line.

The midfielders start from the cone and attack the pole and execute a feint/move left or left before delivering a long pass into the opposite square cone area.

The forward/winger, must time their run well into the cone square to execute an attempt on goal, which if is scored will be worth 1 point. If the player scores from a volley or header, it will be worth 2 points.

The practise continues with the players' roles exchanging and the opposing team executes the same practise with the left and right foot. After 8 minutes we swap the teams over so everyone uses both feet.

## Coaching Points

1. The midfielder needs to deliver the pass as a lofted pass at the right pace.
2. The forward/winger needs to time and possibly bend their run in order to stay onside and also prevent he pass from going over his head.

# Quick Possession and Transition Play to the Striker

**20 Minutes**

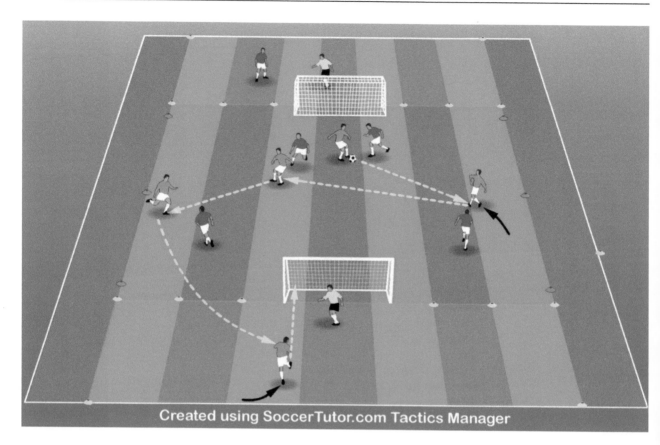

Created using SoccerTutor.com Tactics Manager

## Objective

To develop quick possession play and quick transitioning to the lone striker.

## Description

In a 50 x 30 yard area we play 4 v 4 with each side having 1 player in a neutral endzone with a goal and goalkeeper.

The teams must complete 5 successful passes before playing a lofted pass to their team-mate (forward / striker) in the neutral zone.

The forward has a maximum of 2 touches to take a shot on goal. If a goal is scored from 1 touch it will count as 2 goals.

## Coaching Points

1.  Body shape should be open on half-turn to see all players.
2.  If marked, create space to get away from marker
3.  Must play quickly with one or two touches
4.  The players should have their heads up and be aware of the position of their forward player.
5.  If volleying, head should be over the ball to keep the shot down.

# Tactical Flank Play, Crossing and Finishing in a SSG

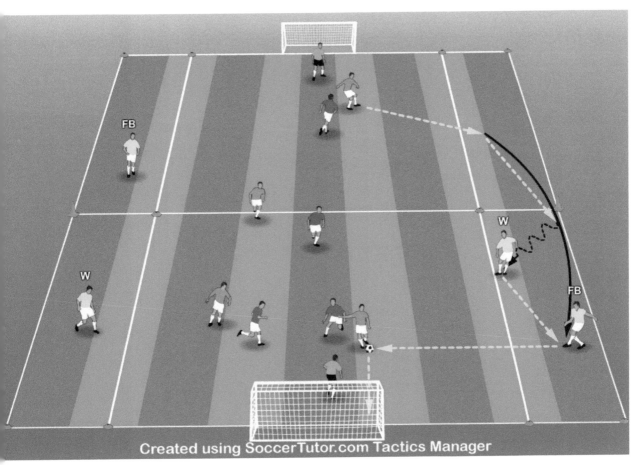

Created using SoccerTutor.com Tactics Manager

**Example 1**

## Objective
To develop tactical flank play with overlaps and quick interchange as well as crossing and finishing.

## Description
In a 60 x 40 yard area or as big as half a pitch we play 4 v 4 with 4 extra wide players who play with the team in possession.

The players within the field play a normal game and aim to use the wide players to create a numerical advantage. The wide players may only receive the ball in their specific zones.

In this diagram the outside full back passes to the winger who dribbles inside to create space for the full back to make an overlapping run.

The winger then plays a pass into the path of the full back who crosses the ball for the team in possession to score.

If a goal is scored from 1 touch it will count as double.

# Tactical Flank Play, Crossing and Finishing in a SSG

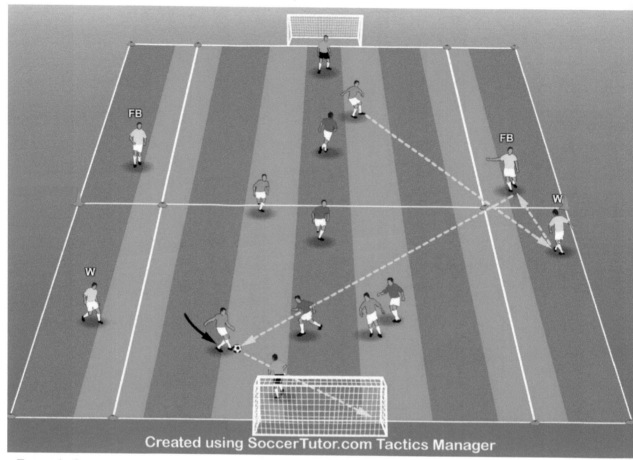

Created using SoccerTutor.com Tactics Manager

**Example 2**

## Description

In this second example the full back makes a pass up the touch-line for the winger who lays the ball back with one touch for the full back to run onto.

The full back crosses the ball from deep for the team in possession to attack and score.

If a goal is scored from 1 touch it will count as double.

## Coaching Points

1. In the 1st diagram, the winger must dribble inside to create space for the overlapping full back.
2. The full back should communicate to the the wide player when to release the pass on the overlap so the pass is in front.
3. In the 2nd diagram the winger's pass/lay-off back to the full back should be at the right amount of pace so the full back can deliver a first time cross.
4. Players inside should look to quickly switch the play to the wide players.
5. Attacking players should time the runs well and attack the ball on the run.

# Session 10

Practice 1   Warm-Up - Transition Play and Heading SSG

Practice 2   Aerobic Conditioning in a Small Sided Game

Practice 3   Heading Finishing Accuracy

Practice 4   Psycho-Kinetics Dynamic Attacking Game

Practice 5   3 v 3 Quick Combinations and Finishing in
the Box

Practice 6   Fast Breakaway Small Sided Game

# Warm-Up - Transition Play and Heading SSG

**15 Minutes**

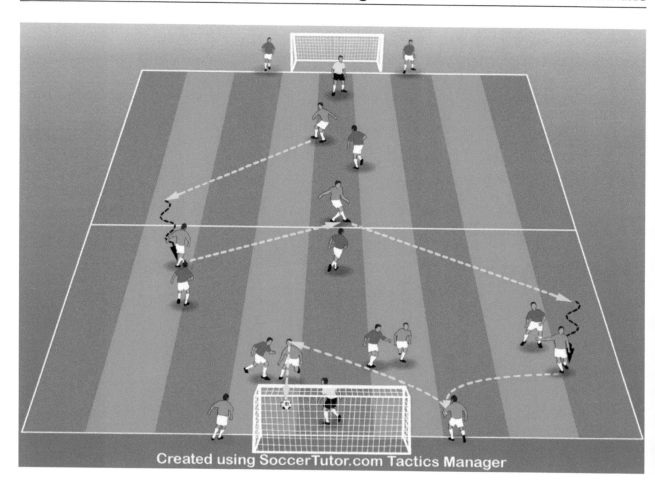

Created using SoccerTutor.com Tactics Manager

## Objective

To develop possession, transition play, finishing with the head.

## Description

In a field area of 40 x 30 yards we play 6 v 6 with each side having 2 extra external players at the end of the pitch either side of the opposition's goal. The external players only use their hands with the aim of throwing the ball to team-mates to head at goal.

The team in possession attacks with an 8 v 6 numerical advantage and should aim to make the transition to the external players as soon as possible.

A goal counts as double if the ball is supplied by an external player and worth triple if combined with a header.

## Coaching Points

1. Make the transition to the external players as soon as possible.
2. Make supportive runs to near, middle and far post to head on goal.

## Aerobic Conditioning in a Small Sided Game

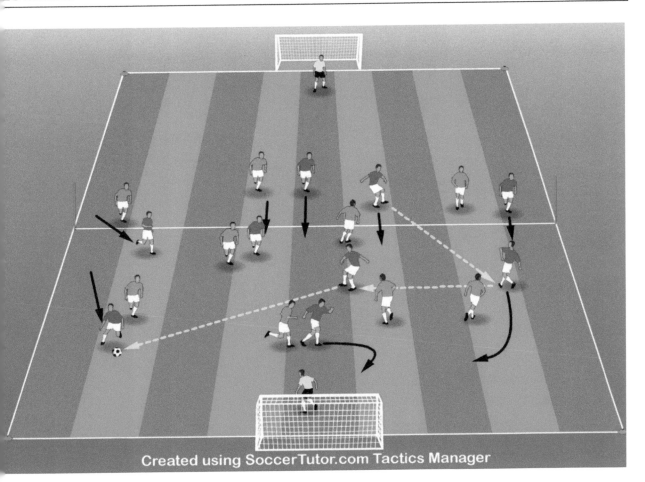

Created using SoccerTutor.com Tactics Manager

## Objective
Develop football specific aerobic conditioning in a quick conditioned small sided game.

## Description
In a field area of 50 x 35 yards we play 10 v 10. If you haven't got that many players, then simply play with the numbers you have, I.e. 7 v 7 etc.

The players are limited to 2 touches in a high tempo match.

All players must be moving at all times.

To score, players must be over the half-way line.

## Coaching Points
1. The players must be continuously moving to replicate the physical movements as in a real game.

## Heading Finishing Accuracy

15 Minutes

Created using SoccerTutor.com Tactics Manager

## Objective

To develop finishing accuracy with the head.

## Description

The goal is divided using boundary poles or tape. A player positioned beside the goal throws the ball into the box for a team-mate to head at goal about 8 yards out.

The player should first head straight into the near post corner and then practice angling his neck to head into the far post. The players can then practice heading at full leap and diving headers.

## Coaching Points

1. Keep eye's open until the moment of impact.
2. Follow through with the forehead the same direction where the headers aimed at.
3. Control the correct use of both arms (before to connecting with the ball, during and after).

20 Minutes

## Psycho-Kinetics Dynamic Attacking Game

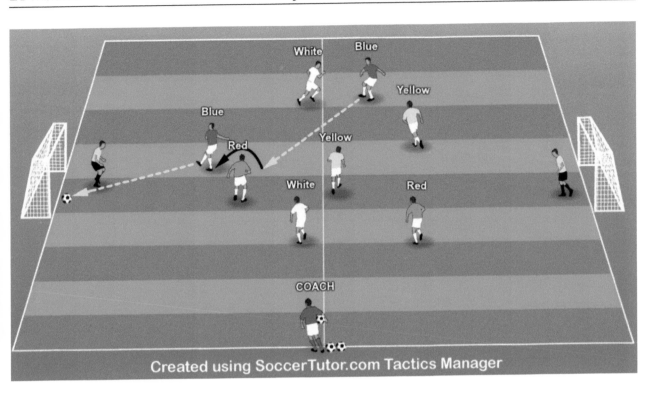

Created using SoccerTutor.com Tactics Manager

## Objective
To develop attacking quick play using Psycho-Kinetics (Think and Act Quickly).

## Description
In a field area of 35 x 25 yards there are goals at both ends of the pitch. 4 pairs wearing different colour bibs compete against each other to score past the goalkeepers. Teams can score in both goals.

A ball is thrown onto the pitch by the coach at the beginning and every time after a goal or when the ball goes out of play.

When a team scores the amount of goals set as a target by the coach, the team with the least amount of goals is eliminated. The practice concluded with a 2 v 2 situation.

## Coaching Points
1. Encourage players to think and play quickly.
2. Try to shoot on goal at every opportunity.
3. Use both feet to shoot on goal

# 3 v 3 Quick Combinations and Finishing in the Box

20 Minutes

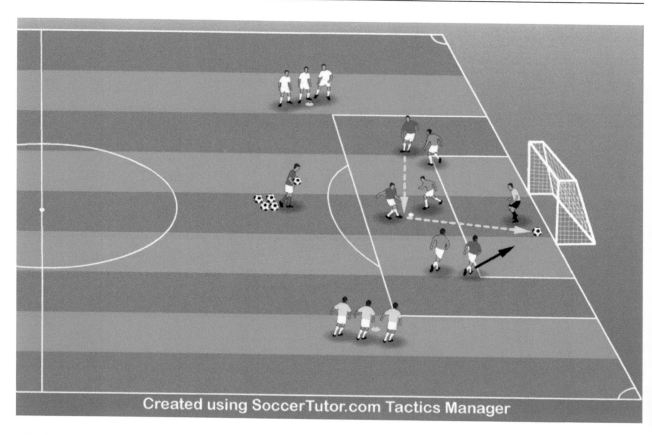

Created using SoccerTutor.com Tactics Manager

## Objective
To develop quick combinations of play with the objective of finishing in the box.

## Description
Inside the penalty area we play 3 v 3. The team that scores a goal remains in the field of play while the other team will swap with another who wait at the edge of the box.

The coach throws the ball in every time the ball leaves the field of play and every time there is a missed shot or goalkeeper's save.

The players should aim to make quick combinations to create space for an attempt on goal.

## Coaching Points
1. Players must try to use 1 touch as often as possible making sure to have fast positive movement.
2. A shot on goal should be realised when half a yard of space is achieved.
3. The play should be of intense speed as the players have time to rest when they are not playing.

## Fast Breakaway Small Sided Game

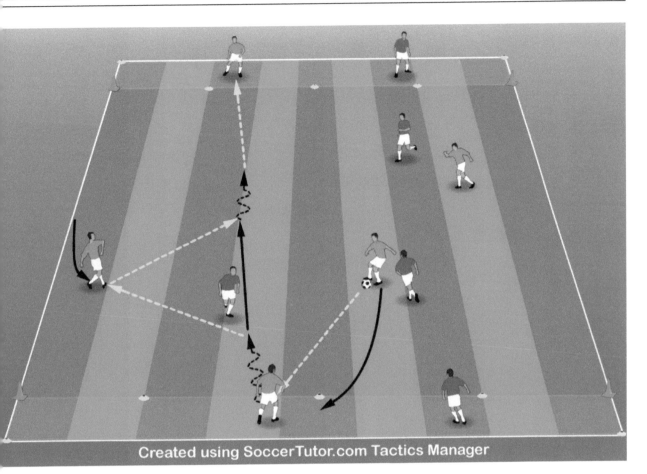

Created using SoccerTutor.com Tactics Manager

## Objective
To develop fast breakaways with quick interchange of positions.

## Description
In a field area of 30 x 30 yards we play 5 v 5. Two target players (one from each team) are placed at opposite ends of the square.

Each team aims to pass the ball to their target players. When a player passes to a target player he follows his pass and replaces their position. The target player then enters the field of play and to develop a fast breakaway.

Every time a successful interchange is achieved 1 point is awarded to the team.

## Coaching Points
1. Players need to make fast accurate passes.
2. At start of the breakaway, players need to make supporting angled runs at both left and right side.
3. Quick combinations should be used with passes made into the path of their oncoming team-mates.

# Session 11

Practice 1     Midfielders- Interceptions and 1 v 1's
Practice 2     Global Conditioning - Technical and Speed of Play
Practice 3     Centre Backs - Tactical Defensive Positioning
Practice 4     Game Situation - 3 v 2 Attacking Play
Practice 5     6 v 6 Game Situations - Quick Combinations
               of Play
Practice 6     Speed of Play and Shooting Small Sided Game

15 Minutes

## Midfielders- Interceptions and 1 v 1's

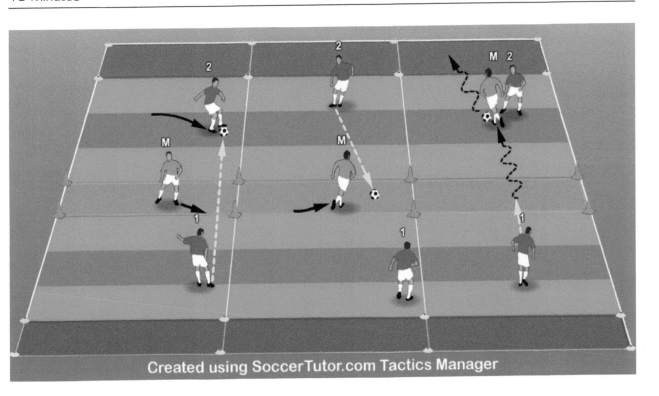

Created using SoccerTutor.com Tactics Manager

## Objective
To develop passing, receiving and midfield interceptions.

## Description
In a field area of 20 x 10 metres players work in groups of 3. The midefielders are positioned in the centre of the pitch in a zone of 2 metres depth.

The players play a 2 v 1 scenario and are limited to 3 touches.

Two players have possession of the ball and aim to pass to each other through the central zone. The central midfield player has the task of intercepting the ball and if successful attempts to dribble the ball past his opponent into the the end-zone.

## Coaching Points
1. Monitor the accuracy and speed of the passing.
2. The player in the central zone needs to close the angle for the player in possession and also anticipate where the pass is going.
3. If the central player intercepts the ball they must make a quick transition to attack and dribble at their opponent using a feint or move.

# Global Conditioning - Technical and Speed of Play

**20 Minutes**

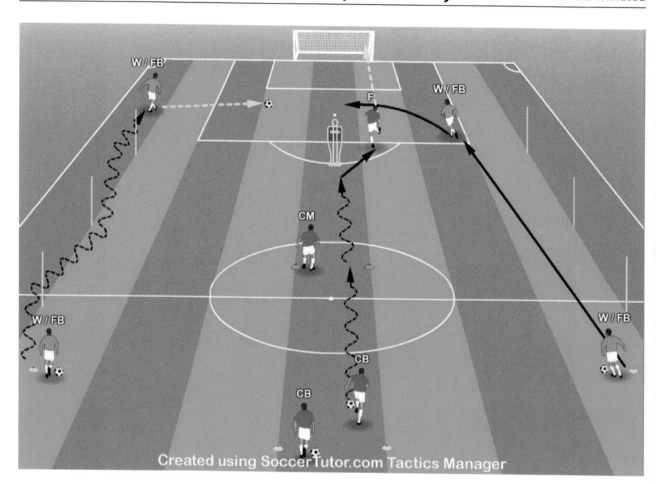

## Objective

To develop player speed and aerobic conditioning as well as developing technical attributes such as ball control, dribbling, RWTB, crossing and shooting.

## Description

Using a two thirds of a pitch, players train in position specific groups to develop their conditioning and well as technical attributes as in game situations.

### On the flanks;

One full back/winger starts by guiding the ball around the poles towards the by-line where they deliver a cross into the box. At the same time, on the opposite full back/winger must time their run to meet the cross and finish on goal.

### In the central zone:

The centre back runs with the ball at a distance of 20 yards before exchanging with the central midfielder or forward who dribbles to the mannequin, executes a feint and shoot on goal.

15 Minutes

## Centre Backs - Tactical Defensive Positioning

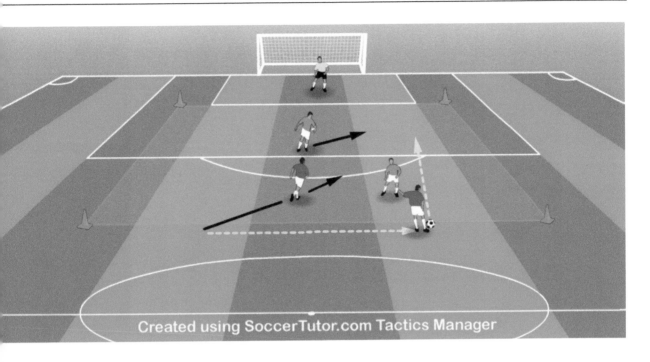

Created using SoccerTutor.com Tactics Manager

## Objective
To develop defensive positioning and movement of the central defenders.

## Description
At a distance of approximately 15 yards outside of the penalty area the 2 attackers exchange passes with the use of only 1 touch.

At the signal of the coach an attacker passes the ball in behind the defenders for the other attacker to run onto.

This is a specific practice for the organisation of the central defenders.

## Coaching Points
1. It is important to teach the central defenders to read the outcome of the pass and the run made by the attacker attempting to get in behind.
2. Pressure - The nearest player goes to the ball and travel while the ball is traveling.
3. Can you win it, intercept the ball, tackle the player, stop player from turning, send player inside/outside.

## Game Situation - 3 v 2 Attacking Play

20 Minutes

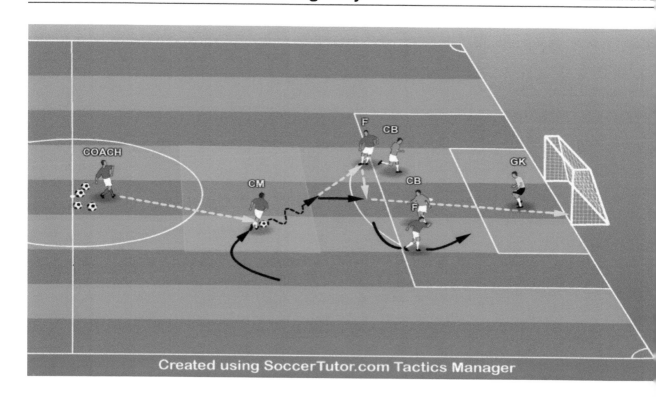

Created using SoccerTutor.com Tactics Manager

## Objective

To develop attacking play and exploiting a numerical advantage.

## Description

In half a pitch we play 3 v 2. Two forwards play with an attacking central midfielder. The coach passes the ball from the half way line to the CM who first must check to create space before receiving the ball into the central zone.

The 3 attacking players must come up with quick combinations between them to create chances to score using the offside rule.

## Coaching Points

1. The centre midfielder needs to create space by checking his run before receiving from the coach and starting the attack.
2. With the numerical advantage, the forwards movement needs to be dynamic to stretch the defence and create gaps to exploit.
3. If there is a clear opportunity to shoot, take it!

15 Minutes

## 6 v 6 Game Situations - Quick Combinations of Play

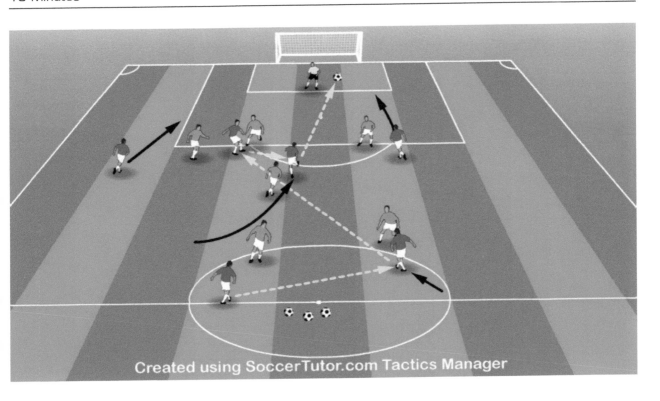

Created using SoccerTutor.com Tactics Manager

### 1. First combination variation

## Objective
To develop combination play starting from deep in midfield.

## Description
In half a pitch we play 6 v 6.

The 2 central midfielders play with one touch and make sideways passes with the opponent midfielders providing passive defensive coverings.

On the coach's signal, play is live and the midfielders must make quick and sharp attacking combinations with team-mates and attempt to finish on target.

# 6 v 6 Game Situations - Quick Combinations of Play

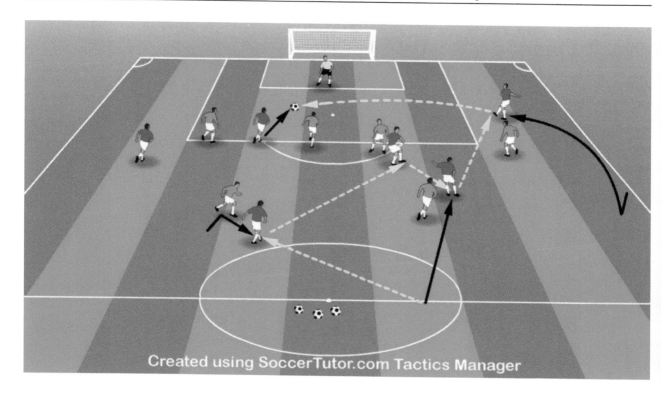

Created using SoccerTutor.com Tactics Manager

**2. Second combination variation**

## Coaching Points
1. Body shape should be open on half-turn to see all players.
2. If marked, create space to get away from marker
3. Must play quickly with one or two touches
4. Movement into space will also create space for teammates to advance into.

20 Minutes

## Speed of Play and Shooting Small Sided Game

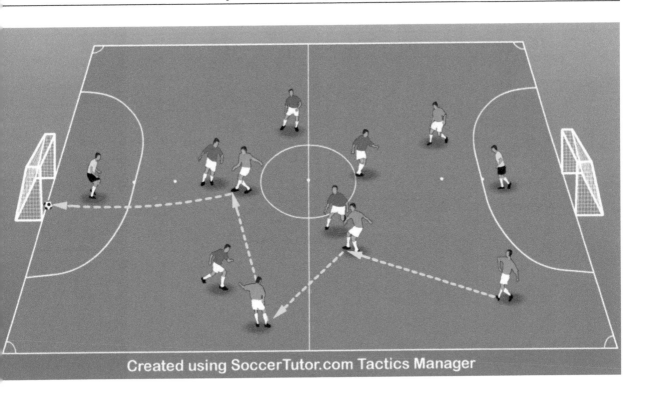

Created using SoccerTutor.com Tactics Manager

## Objective
Develop speed of play to create shooting opportunities.

## Description
In a 40 x 30 yard area we play 5 v 5.

The teams must count the amount of passes they have made and must take a shot on goal before reaching 5 passes.

Each team has the obligation to count the passes. In no more than 5 passes they have to shoot at goal, otherwise they lose the ball possession. The practise stimulates quick direct play and the conclusion to score at goal.

## Coaching Points
1. Players should receive the ball half-turned to speed up the transition to the next pass, dribble or shot on goal.
2. Encourage players to think and play quickly, selecting the right pass before receiving the ball.

# Session 12

Practice 1    Technical Ball Control, Juggling and Volleying

Practice 2    Anaerobic Power with the Ball

Practice 3    1 v 1 Shielding the Ball

Practice 4    2 v 1 Attacking and Defending Game

Practice 5    Psycho-Kinetics (Think and Act Quickly)
              Possession Play

Practice 6    Create Space in a Zonal Small Sided Game

## Technical Ball Control, Juggling and Volleying

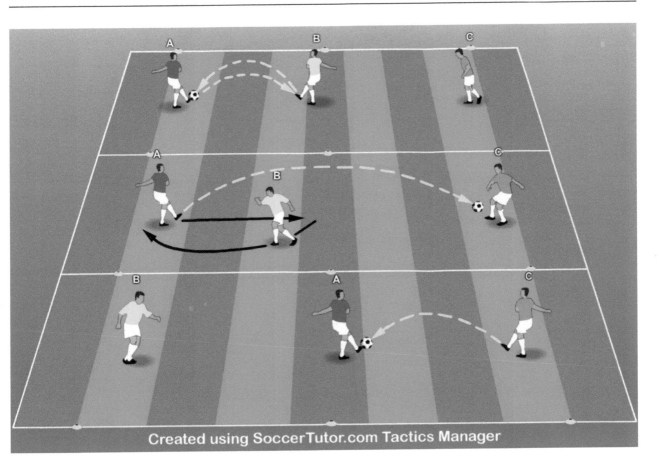

Created using SoccerTutor.com Tactics Manager

## Objective
To develop ball control and lofted volley pass.

## Description
In groups 3 players work with a ball and are limited to 3 touches.

Players A and C are at a distance of about 10 yards from each other.

The practice starts with **Player A** who juggles with the ball and then makes a volley pass to **Player B** in the air who returns the ball back to **Player A**.

**Player A** receives the ball in the air and makes a volley pass to **Player C**. **Players A** and **B** exchange positions. **Player A** runs up to **Player C** and they start the sequence again.

## Coaching Points
Practice of juggling should be encouraged at home as it develops technique and ball control.

# Anaerobic Power with the Ball

15 Minutes

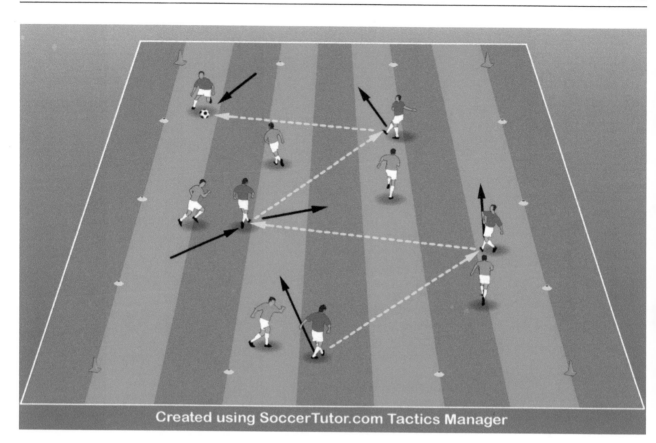

Created using SoccerTutor.com Tactics Manager

## Objective

To develop anaerobic power with possession of the ball.

## Description

In a field area of 30 x 20 yards we play 5 v 5. We have 4 teams. The 2 teams playing must play at an intense level with maximum of 2 touches, keeping possession and working on the power of their acceleration.

The teams play for 4 minutes and then rest for 4 minutes while the other 2 teams are playing.

## Coaching Points

The players must be continuously moving to replicate the fast physical movements as in a real game.

## 1 v 1 Shielding the Ball

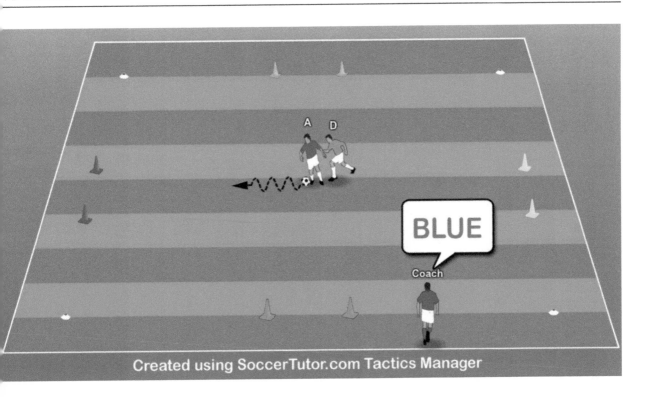

Created using SoccerTutor.com Tactics Manager

## Objective
To develop a player's ability to shield (protect) the ball from a defender and coaching the correct body shape.

## Description
In a field area of 10 x 10 yards there are 2 players (1 attacker and 1 defender).

On the coaches signal the attacker has to shield the ball from the defender for 7-8 seconds. After this time the attacker shoots in 1 of the 4 little coloured goals pointed by the coach who calls the colour to attack.

If the defender manages to recover the ball from the attacker before the colour is called, the roles are reversed.

## Coaching Points
1. The player needs to use their body as a barrier between the defender and the ball making sure to shield the ball at all costs.
2. Arms should be out to feel and block the defender from getting near the ball.
3. Keep the ball moving in the opposite direction to the where defender attempt to challenge.

## 2 v 1 Attacking and Defending Game

20 Minutes

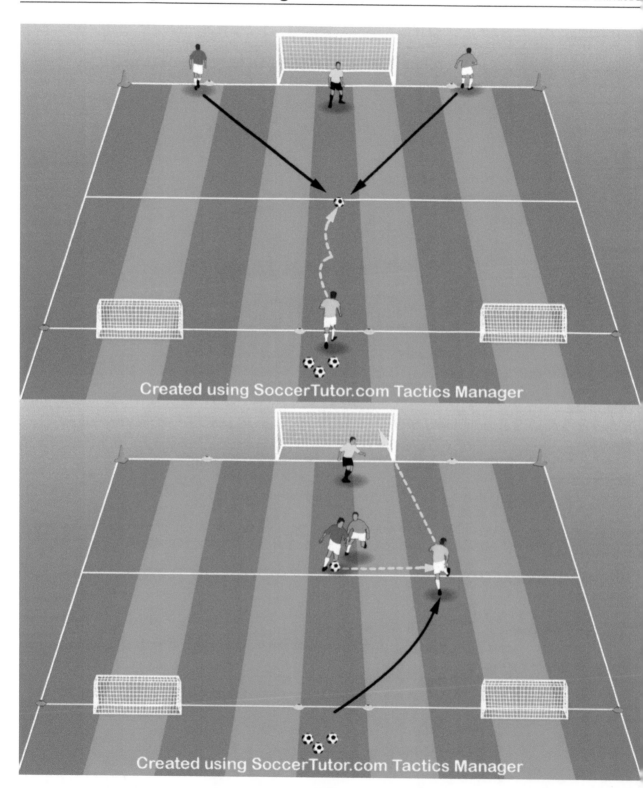

## 2 v 1 Attacking and Defending Game

### Objective
To develop attacking combinations using the numerical advantage of 2 v 1, along with the defender positioning himself correctly.

### Description
In a field area of 30 x 20 yards we work with 3 players at the same time.

2 players are positioned on the goal line with their backs to the ball. An attacking player placed between 2 small goals volleys the ball to the centre of the field.

As soon as the 2 players hear the sound of the ball bouncing they race to the ball. The first to arrive becomes the attacker to create a 2 v 1 situation with the player who passed the ball. The aim is to attack and score in the goal past the goalkeeper.

If the defender retrieves the ball, he can attack either of the 2 empty goals.

### Coaching Points
1. The attacker who receives the ball needs to use his body to block the defender.
2. The attackers should practice 1-2 combinations quickly getting in behind the defender.
3. If there is a clear opportunity to shoot, take it!

# Psycho-Kinetics (Think and Act Quickly) Possession Play

20 Minutes

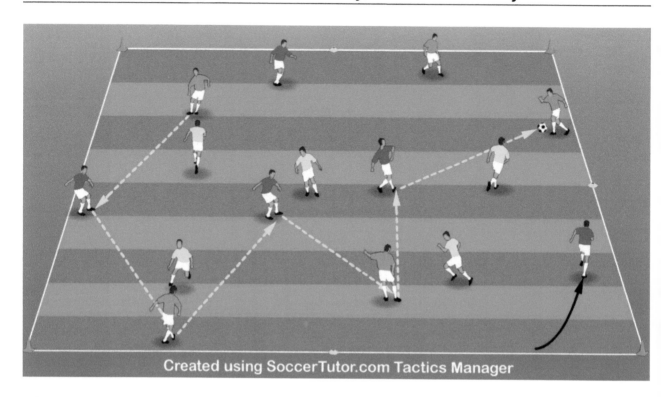

Created using SoccerTutor.com Tactics Manager

## Objective

To develop player passing, possession play and to think and act quickly using Psycho Kinetics.

## Description

In a field area of 25 x 25 yards we play with 3 colour teams of 5 players. 2 teams play together (e.g. Blues plays with Whites against the Yellows) to create a situation of 10 v 5.

A point is scored when the 2 teams complete 10 consecutive passes. Every two minutes the teams exchange roles.

### Variation

To remove the requirement of achieving 10 passes to simply maintaining possession. When the defending team regains possession they aim to then maintain the ball with one of the other teams.

## Coaching Points

1. Open body shape to see all of the playing options.
2. Play quickly (maximum of two touches) considering the overload of players.
3. If needed, create space to get away from the marker

## Create Space in a Zonal Small Sided Game

Created using SoccerTutor.com Tactics Manager

## Objective
To coach tactical play for specific roles and positions.

## Description
In a field area of 35 x 25 yards we play with 8 v 8 with 2 goalkeepers. We divide the field into 3 sections; Defence, Midfield and Attack.

In the Defensive section we play with a maximum of 2 touches
In the Midfield section we play with a maximum of 3 touches.
In the Attacking third the players play with unlimited touches.

In each section we can create numerical advantage to encourage overlaps and penetrative play. For example if a midfielder plays to an attacker, he can enter the attacking zone to create a numerical advantage.

## Coaching Points
1. Running into space to receive the ball, fully exploiting the numerical advantage in certain areas as well as third-man runs and overlaps.

## Create Space in a Zonal Small Sided Game

2. Movement of players and passing must be done as quickly as possible.
3. Correct body shape (open on the half-turn) and positioning is important to know where the next pass is going.
4. The defenders must develop good communication and close down together, pressing the side in possession.

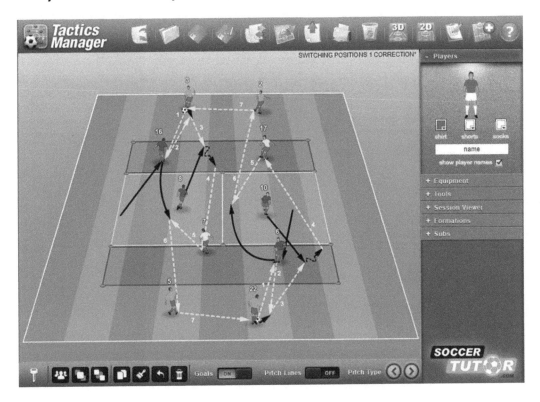